Slavery

WILLIAM ELLERY CHANNING

University Printing House, Cambridge, CB2 8BS, United Kingdom

Published in the United States of America by Cambridge University Press, New York

Cambridge University Press is part of the University of Cambridge.
It furthers the University's mission by disseminating knowledge in the pursuit of
education, learning and research at the highest international levels of excellence.

www.cambridge.org
Information on this title: www.cambridge.org/9781108053150

© in this compilation Cambridge University Press 2013

This edition first published 1836
This digitally printed version 2013

ISBN 978-1-108-05315-0 Paperback

SLAVERY.

BY

WILLIAM E. CHANNING.

———

REPRINTED FROM THE BOSTON (U. S,) EDITION.

LONDON:
PUBLISHED BY ROWLAND HUNTER,
ST. PAUL'S CHURCH-YARD.
———
MDCCCXXXVI.
PRICE EIGHTEEN-PENCE.

BIRMINGHAM:
EDWARD C. OSBORNE,
TEMPLE ROW.

CONTENTS.

INTRODUCTION.

THE first question to be proposed by a rational being is, not what is profitable, but what is Right. Duty must be primary, prominent, most conspicuous, among the objects of human thought and pursuit. If we cast it down from its supremacy, if we inquire first for our interests and then for our duties, we shall certainly err. We can never see the Right clearly and fully, but by making it our first concern. No judgment can be just or wise, but that which is built on the conviction of the paramount worth and importance of Duty. This is the fundamental truth, the supreme law of reason; and the mind, which does not start from this in its inquiries into human affairs, is doomed to great, perhaps fatal error.

The Right is the supreme good, and includes all other goods. In seeking and adhering to it, we secure our true and only happiness. All prosperity, not founded on it, is built on sand. If human affairs are controlled, as we believe, by Almighty Rectitude and Impartial Goodness, then to hope for happiness from wrong doing is as insane as to seek health and prosperity by rebelling against the laws of nature, by sowing our seed on the ocean, or making poison our common food. There is but one unfailing good; and that is, fidelity to the Everlasting Law written on the heart, and rewritten and republished in God's Word.

Whoever places this faith in the everlasting law of rectitude must of course regard the question of slavery first and chiefly as a moral question. All other considerations will weigh little with him, compared with its moral character and moral influences. The following remarks, therefore, are designed to aid the reader in forming a just moral judgment of slavery. Great truths, inalienable rights, everlasting duties, these will form the chief subjects of this discussion. There are times when the assertion of great principles is the best service a man can render society. The present is a moment of bewildering excitement, when men's minds are stormed and dark-

A

ened by strong passions and fierce conflicts; and also a moment of absorbing worldliness, when the moral law is made to bow to expediency, and its high and strict requirements are decried or dismissed as metaphysical abstractions, or impracticable theories. At such a season, to utter great principles without passion, and in the spirit of unfeigned and universal good-will, and to engrave them deeply and durably on men's minds, is to do more for the world, than to open mines of wealth, or to frame the most successful schemes of policy.

Of late our country has been convulsed by the question of slavery; and the people, in proportion as they have felt vehemently, have thought superficially, or hardly thought at all; and we see the results in a singular want of well defined principles, in a strange vagueness and inconsistency of opinion, and in the proneness to excess which belongs to unsettled minds. The multitude have been called, now to contemplate the horrors of slavery, and now to shudder at the ruin and bloodshed which must follow emancipation. The word Massacre has resounded through the land, striking terror into strong as well as tender hearts, and awakening indignation against whatever may seem to threaten such a consummation. The consequence is, that not a few dread all discussion of the subject and if not reconciled to the continuance of slavery, at least believe that they have no duty to perform, no testimony to bear, no influence to exert, no sentiments to cherish and spread, in relation to this evil. What is still worse, opinions either favoring or extenuating it are heard with little or no disapprobation. Concessions are made to it which would once have shocked the community; whilst to assail it is pronounced unwise and perilous. No stronger reason for a calm exposition of its true character can be given, than this very state of the public mind. A community can suffer no greater calamity than the loss of its principles. Lofty and pure sentiment is the life and hope of a people. There was never such an obligation to discuss slavery as at this moment, when recent events have done much to unsettle and obscure men's minds in regard to it. This result is to be ascribed in part to the injudicious vehemence of those who have taken into their hands the care of the slave. Such ought to remember that to espouse a good cause is not enough. We must maintain it in a spirit answering to its dignity. Let no man touch the great interest of humanity, who does not strive to sanctify himself for the work by cleansing his heart of all wrath and uncharitableness, who cannot hope that he is in a measure baptised unto the spirit of universal love. Even sympathy with the injured and oppressed may do harm, by being partial, exclusive, and bitterly indignant. How far the declension of the spirit of freedom is to be ascribed to the cause now suggested I do not say. The effect is plain, and whoever sees and laments the evil should strive to arrest it.

Slavery ought to be discussed. We ought to think, feel, speak, and write about it. But whatever we do in regard to it should be done with a deep feeling of responsibility, and so done as not to put in jeopardy the peace of the slave-holding States. On this point public opinion has not been and cannot be too strongly pronounced. Slavery, indeed, from its very nature, must be a ground of alarm wherever it exists. Slavery and security can by no device be joined together. But we may not, must not, by rashness and passion increase the peril. To instigate the slave to insurrection is a crime for which no rebuke and no punishment can be too severe. This would be to involve slave and master in common ruin. It is not enough to say, that the Constitution is violated by any action endangering the slave-holding portion of our country. A higher law than the Constitution forbids this unholy interference. Were our national union dissolved, we ought to reprobate, as sternly as we now do, the slightest manifestation of a disposition to stir up a servile war. Still more, were the free and the slave-holding States not only separated, but engaged in the fiercest hostilities, the former would deserve the abhorrence of the world, and the indignation of Heaven, were they to resort to insurrection and massacre as means of victory. Better were it for us to bare our own breasts to the knife of the slave, than to arm him with it against his master.

It is not by personal, direct action on the mind of the slave that we can do him good. Our concern is with the free. With the free we are to plead his cause. And this is peculiarly our duty, because we have bound ourselves to resist his efforts for his own emancipation. We suffer him to do nothing for himself. The more, then, should be done for him. Our physical power is pledged against him in case of revolt. Then our moral power should be exerted for his relief. His weakness, which we increase, gives him a claim to the only aid we can afford, to our moral sympathy, to the free and faithful exposition of his wrongs. As men, as Christians, as citizens, we have duties to the slave, as well as to every other member of the community. On this point we have no liberty. The Eternal Law binds us to take the side of the injured; and this law is peculiarly obligatory, when we forbid him to lift an arm in his own defence.

Let it not be said we can do nothing for the slave. We can do much. We have a power mightier than armies, the power of truth, of principle, of virtue, of right, of religion, of love. We have a power, which is growing with every advance of civilization, before which the slave-trade has fallen, which is mitigating the sternest despotisms, which is spreading education through all ranks of society, which is bearing Christianity to the ends of the earth, which carries in itself the pledge of destruction to every institution which debases humanity. Who can measure the power of Christian philanthropy, of enlightened goodness, pouring itself forth in prayers and persuasions, from the press and pulpit, from the lips and hearts of devoted men, and more and more binding together the wise and good in the cause of their race? All other powers may fail. This must triumph. It is leagued with God's omnipotence. It is God himself acting in the hearts of his children. It has an ally in every conscience, in every human breast, in the wrong doer himself. This spirit has but begun its work on earth. It is breathing itself more and more through literature, education, institutions and opinion. Slavery cannot stand before it. Great moral principles, pure and generous sentiments, cannot be confined to this or that spot. They cannot be shut out by territorial lines, or local legislation. They are divine inspirations, and partake of the omnipresence of their Author. The deliberate, solemn conviction of good men through the world, that slavery is a grievous wrong to human nature, will make itself felt. To increase this moral power is every man's duty. To embody and express this great truth is in every man's power; and thus every man can do something to break the chain of the slave.

There are not a few persons, who, from vulgar modes of thinking, cannot be interested in this subject. Because the slave is a degraded being, they think slavery a low topic, and wonder how it can excite the attention and sympathy of those who can discuss or feel for any thing else. Now the truth is, that slavery, regarded only in a philosophical light, is a theme worthy of the highest minds. It involves the gravest questions about human nature and society. It carries us into the problems which have exercised for ages the highest understandings. It calls us to inquire into the foundation, nature, and extent of human rights, into the distinction between a person and a thing, into the true relations of man and man, into the obligations of the community to each of its members into the the the ground and laws of property, and above all into the true dignity and indestructable claims of a moral being. I venture to say, there is no subject, now agitated by the community, which can compare in philosophical dignity with slavery; and yet to multitudes the question falls under the same contempt with the slave himself. To many, a writer seems to lower himself who touches it. The falsely refined, who want intellectual force to grasp it, pronounce it unworthy of their notice.

But this subject has more than philosophical dignity. It has an important bearing on character. Our interest in it is one test by which our comprehension of the distinctive spirit of Christianity must be judged. Christianity is the manifestation and inculcation of Universal Love. The great teaching of Christianity is, that we must recognise and respect human nature in all its forms, in the poorest, most ignorant, most fallen. We must look beneath "the flesh," to " the spirit." The Spiritual principle in a man is what entitles him to our brotherly regard. To be just to this is the great injunction of our religion. To overlook this, on account of condition or color, is to violate the great Christian law. We have reason to think that it is one design of God, in appointing the vast diversities of human condition, to put to the test and to bring out most distinctly the principle of love. It is wisely ordered, that human nature is not set before us in a few forms of beauty, magnificence, and outward glory. To be dazzled and attracted by these would be no sign of reverence for what is interior and spiritual in human nature. To lead us to discern and love this, we are brought into connexion with fellow-creatures, whose outward circumstances are repulsive. To recognise our own spiritual nature and God's image in these humble forms, to recognise as brethren those who want all outward distinctions, is the chief way in which we are to manifest the spirit of Him, who came to raise the fallen and to save the lost. We see, then, the moral importance of the question of slavery; according to our decision of it, we determine our comprehension of the Christian law. He who cannot see a brother, a child of God, a man possessing all the rights of humanity under a skin darker than his own, wants the vision of a Christian. He worships the Outward. The Spirit is not yet revealed to him. To look unmoved on the degradation and wrongs of a fellow-creature, because burned by a fiercer sun, proves us strangers to justice and love, in those universal forms which characterize Christianity. The greatest of all distinctions, the only enduring one, is moral goodness, virtue, religion. Outward distinctions cannot add to the dignity of this. The wealth of worlds is " not sufficient for a burnt offering" on its altar. A being capable of this is invested by God with solemn claims on his fellow-creatures. To exclude millions of such beings from our sympathy, because of outward disadvantages, proves, that, in whatever else we surpass them, we are not their superiors in Christian virtue.

The spirit of Christianity, I have said, is distinguished by Universality. It is universal justice. It respects all the rights of all beings. It suffers no being, however obscure, to be wronged, without condemning the wrong doer. Impartial, uncompromising, fearless, it screens no favorites, is dazzled by no power, spreads its shield over the weakest, summons the mightiest to its bar, and speaks to the conscience in tones, under which the mightiest have quailed. It is also universal love, comprehending those that are near and those that are afar off, the high and the low, the rich and poor, descending to the fallen, and especially binding itself to those in whom human nature is trampled under foot. Such is the spirit of Christianity; and nothing but the illumination of this spirit can prepare us to pass judgment on slavery.

These remarks are intended to show the spirit in which slavery ought to be approached, and the point of view from which it will be regarded in the present discussion. My plan may be briefly sketched.

1. I shall show that man cannot be justly held and used as Property.

2. I shall show that man has sacred and infallible rights, of which slavery is the infraction.

3. I shall offer some explanations to prevent misapplication of these principles.

4. I shall unfold the evils of slavery.

5. I shall consider the argument which the Scriptures are thought to furnish in favor of slavery.

6. I shall offer some remarks on the means of removing it.

7. I shall offer some remarks on abolitionism.

8. I shall conclude with a few reflections on the duties belonging to the times.

In the first two sections I propose to show that slavery is a great wrong, but I do not intend to pass sentence on the character of the slave-holder. These two subjects are distinct. Men are not always to be interpreted by their acts or institutions. The same acts in different circumstances admit and even require very different constructions. I offer this remark, that the subject may be approached without prejudice or personal reference. The single object is to settle great principles. Their bearing on individuals will be a subject of distinct consideration.

CHAPTER I.

PROPERTY.

THE slave-holder claims the slave as his Property. The very idea of a slave is, that he belongs to another, that he is bound to live and labor for another, to be another's instrument, and to make another's will his habitual law, however adverse to his own. Another owns him, and of course has a right to his time and strength, a right to the fruits of his labor, a right to task him without his consent, and to determine the kind and duration of his toil, a right to confine him to any bounds, a right to extort the required work by stripes, a right, in a word, to use him as a tool, without contract, against his will, and in denial of his right to dispose of himself or to use his power for his own good. "A slave," says the Louisiana Code, "is in the power of his master to whom he belongs. The master may sell him, dispose of his person, his industry, his labor; he can do nothing, possess nothing, nor acquire any thing, but which must belong to his master." "Slaves shall be deemed, taken, reputed, and adjudged," say the South Carolina laws, "to be chattels personal in the hands of their masters, and possessions to all intents and purposes whatsoever." Such is slavery, a claim to man as property.

Now this claim of property in a human being is altogether false, groundless. No such right of man in man can exist. A human being cannot be justly owned. To hold and treat him as property is to inflict a great wrong, to incur the guilt of oppression.

This position there is a difficulty in maintaining on account of its exceeding obviousness. It is too plain for proof. To defend it is like trying to confirm a self-evident truth. To find arguments is not easy, because an argument is something clearer than the proposition to be sustained. The man, who, on hearing the claim to property in man, does not see and feel distinctly that it is a cruel usurpation, is hardly to be reached by reasoning, for it is hard to find any plainer principles than what he begins with denying. I will endeavour, however, to illustrate the truth which I have stated.

1. It is plain, that, if one man may be held as property, then every man may be so held. If there be nothing in human nature, in our common nature, which excludes and forbids the conversion of him who possesses it into an article of property; if the right of the free to liberty is founded, not on their essential attributes as rational and moral beings, but on certain adventitious, accidental circumstances, into which they have been thrown; then every human being, by a change of circumstances, may justly be held and treated by another as property. If one man may be rightfully reduced to slavery, then there is not a human being on whom the same chain may not be imposed. Now let every reader ask himself this plain question: Could I, can I, be rightfully seized, and made an article of property; be made a passive instrument of another's will and pleasure; be subjected to another's irresponsible power; be subjected to stripes at another's will; be denied the control and use of my own limbs and faculties for my own good? Does any man so questioned, doubt, waver, look about him for an answer? Is not the reply given immediately, intuitively, by his whole inward being? Does not an unhesitating, unerring conviction spring up in my breast, that no other man can acquire such a right in myself? Do we not repel indignantly and with horror the thought of being reduced to the condition of tools and chattels to a fellow-creature? Is there any moral truth more deeply rooted in us, than that such a degradation would be an infinite wrong? And if this impression be a delusion, on what single moral conviction can we rely? This deep assurance, that we cannot be rightfully made another's property, does not rest on the hue of our skins, or the place of our birth, or our strength, or wealth. These things do not enter our thoughts. The consciousness of indestructible right, is a part of our moral being. The consciousness of our humanity involves the persuasion, that we cannot be owned as a tree or a brute. As men we cannot justly be

made slaves. Then no man can be rightfully enslaved. In casting the yoke from ourselves as an unspeakable wrong, we condemn ourselves as wrongdoers and oppressors in laying it on any who share our nature. It is not necessary to inquire whether a man, by extreme guilt, may not forfeit the right of his nature, and be justly punished with slavery. On this point crude notions prevail. But the discussion would be foreign to the present subject. We are now not speaking of criminals. We speak of innocent men, who have given us no hold on them by guilt; and our own consciousness is a proof, that such cannot rightfully be seized as property by a fellow-creature.

2. A man cannot be seized and held as property, because he has Rights. What these rights are, whether few or many, or whether all men have the same, are questions for future discussion. All that is assumed now is, that every human being has *some* rights. This truth cannot be denied, but by denying to a portion of the race that moral nature which is the sure and only foundation of rights. This truth has never, I believe, been disputed. It is even recongnised in the very codes of slave-legislation, which, while they strip a man of liberty, affirm his right to life, and threaten his murderer with punishment. Now, I say a being having rights cannot justly be made property; for this claim over him virtually annuls all his rights. It strips him of all power to assert them. It makes it a crime to assert them. The very essence of slavery is, to put a man defenceless into the hands of another. The right claimed by the master, to task, to force, to imprison, to whip, and to punish the slave at discretion, and especially to prevent the least resistance to his will, is a virtual denial and subversion of all the rights of the victim of his power. The two cannot stand together. Can we doubt which of them ought to fall?

3. Another argument against property is to be found in the Essential Equality of men. I know that this doctrine, so venerable in the eyes of our fathers, has lately been denied. Verbal logicians have told us that men are "born equal," only in the sense of being equally born. They have asked

whether all are equally tall, strong, or beautiful; or whether
nature, Procrustes-like, reduces all her children to one stan-
dard of intellect and virtue. By such arguments it is attempted to set aside the principle of equality, on which the
soundest moralists have reared the structure of social duty;
and in these ways the old foundations of despotic power, which
our fathers in their simplicity thought they had subverted, are
laid again by their sons.

It is freely granted, that there are innumerable diversities
among men; but be it remembered, they are ordained to bind
men together, and not to subdue one to the other; ordained
to give means and occasions of mutual aid, and to carry forward each and all, so that the good of all is equally intended
in this distribution of various gifts. Be it also remembered,
that these diversities among men are as nothing in comparison
with the attributes in which they agree, and it is this which
constitutes their essential equality. All men have the same
rational nature, and the same power of conscience, and all
are equally made for indefinite improvement of these divine
faculties, and for the happiness to be found in their virtuous
use. Who, that comprehends these gifts, does not see that
the diversities of the race vanish before them? Let it be
added, that the natural advantages, which distinguish one
man from another, are so bestowed as to counterbalance one
another, and bestowed with regard to rank or condition in
life. Whoever surpasses in one endowment is inferior in
others. Even genius, the greatest gift, is found in union
with strange infirmities, and often places its possessors below
ordinary men in the conduct of life. Great learning is often
put to shame by the mother-wit and keen good sense of uneducated men. Nature, indeed, pays no heed to birth or condition in bestowing her favors. The noblest spirits sometimes
grow up in the obscurest spheres. Thus equal are men; and
among these equals, who can substantiate his claim to make
others his property, his tools, the mere instruments of his
private interest and gratification? Let this claim begin, and
where will it stop? If one may assert it, why not all? Among
these partakers of the same rational and moral nature, who
can make good a right over others, which others may not es-
tablish over himself? Does he insist on superior strength of

body or mind? Who of us has no superior in one or the other of these endowments? Is it sure that the slave or the slave's child may not surpass his master in intellectual energy or in moral worth? Has nature conferred distinctions which tell us plainly, who shall be owners and who be owned? Who of us can unblushingly lift his head and say that God has written "master" there? or who can show the word "slave" engraven on his brother's brow? The equality of nature makes slavery a wrong. Nature's seal is affixed to no instrument, by which property in a single human being is conveyed.

4. That a human being cannot be justly held and used as property is apparent from the very nature of property. Property is an exclusive, single right. It shuts out all claim but that of the possessor. What one man owns, cannot belong to another. What, then, is the consequence of holding a human being as property? Plainly this. He can have no right to himself. His limbs are, in truth, not morally his own. He has not a right to his own strength. It belongs to another. His will, intellect, and muscles, all the powers of body and mind which are exercised in labor, he is bound to regard as another's. Now, if there be property in any thing, it is that of a man in his own person, mind, and strength. All other rights are weak, unmeaning, compared with this, and in denying this all right is denied. It is true that an individual may forfeit by crime his right to the use of his limbs, and even to his life. But the very idea of forfeiture implies that the right was originally possessed. It is true that a man may by contract give to another a limited right to his strength. But he gives only because he possesses it, and gives it for considerations which he deems beneficial to himself; and the right conferred ceases at once on violation of the conditions on which it was bestowed. To deny the right of a human being to himself, to his own limbs and faculties, to his energy of body and mind, is an absurdity too gross to be confuted by any thing but a simple statement. Yet this absurdity is involved in the idea of his belonging to another.

5. We have a plain recognition of the principle now laid down, in the universal indignation excited towards a man

who makes another his slave. Our laws know no higher crime than that of reducing a man to slavery. To steal or to buy an African on his own shores is piracy. In this act the greatest wrong is inflicted, the most sacred right violated. But if a human being cannot without infinite injustice be seized as property, then he cannot without equal wrong be held and used as such. The wrong in the first seizure lies in the destination of a human being to future bondage, to the criminal use of him as a chattel or brute. Can that very use, which makes the original seizure an enormous wrong, become gradually innocent? If the slave receive injury without measure at the first moment of the outrage, is he less injured by being held fast the second or the third? Does the duration of wrong, the increase of it by continuance, convert it into right? It is true, in many cases, that length of possession is considered as giving a right, where the goods were acquired by unlawful means. But in these cases the goods were such as might justly be appropriated to individual use. They were intended by the Creator to be owned. They fulfil their purpose by passing into the hands of an exclusive possessor. It is essential to rightful property in a thing, that the thing from its nature may be rightfully appropriated. If it cannot originally be made one's own without crime, it certainly cannot be continued as such without guilt. Now, the ground, on which the seizure of the African on his own shore is condemned, is, that he is a Man, who has by his nature a right to be free. Ought not, then, the same condemnation to light on the continuance of his yoke? Still more. Whence is it that length of possession is considered by the laws as conferring a right? I answer, from the difficulty of determining the original proprietor, and from the apprehension of unsettling all property by carrying back inquiry beyond a certain time. Suppose, however, an article of property to be of such a nature that it could bear the name of the true original owner, stamped on it in bright and indelible characters. In this case, the whole ground, on which length of possession bars other claims, would fail. The proprietor would not be concealed or rendered doubtful by the lapse of time. Would not he, who should receive such an article from a robber or a succession of robbers, be involved in their guilt? Now, the true owner of a human being is made manifest to all. It is Himself. No brand on the slave was ever so conspicuous as the mark of property which God has set on him. God, in making him a rational and moral being, has put a glorious stamp upon him, which all the slave-legislation and slave-markets of worlds cannot efface. Hence no right accrues to the master from the length of the wrong which has been done to the slave.

6. Another argument against the right of property in man may be drawn from a very obvious principle of moral science. It is a plain truth, universally received, that every right supposes or involves a corresponding Obligation. If, then a man has a right to another's person or powers, the latter is under obligation to give himself up as a chattel to the former. This is his duty. He is bound to be a slave; and bound not merely by the Christian law which enjoins submission to injury, not merely by prudential considerations, or by the claims of public order and peace; but bound because another has a right of Ownership, has a Moral claim to him, so that he would be guilty of dishonesty, of robbery, in withdrawing himself from this other's service. It is his Duty to work for his master, though all compulsion were withdrawn; and in deserting him he would commit the crime of taking away another man's property, as truly as if he were to carry off his owner's purse. Now, do we not instantly feel, can we help feeling, that this is false? Is the slave thus morally bound? When the African was first brought to these shores, would he have violated a solemn obligation, by slipping his chain, and flying back to his native home? Would he not have been bound to seize the precious opportunity of escape? Is the slave under a moral obligation to confine himself, his wife, and children, to a spot where their union in a moment may be forcibly dissolved? Ought he not, if he can, to place himself and his family under the guardianship of equal laws? Should we blame him for leaving his yoke? Do we not feel, that, in the same condition, a sense of duty would quicken our flying steps? Where, then, is the obligation which would necessarily be imposed, if the right existed which the master claims? The absence of obligation proves the want of the right. The claim is groundless. It is a cruel wrong.

7. I come now to what is to my own mind the great argu-

ment against seizing and using a man as property. He cannot be property in the sight of God and justice, because he is a Rational, Moral, Immortal Being; because created in God's image, and therefore in the highest sense his child; because created to unfold Godlike faculties, and to govern himself by a Divine Law written on his heart, and republished in God's Word. His whole nature forbids that he should be seized as property. From his very nature it follows, that so to seize him is to offer an insult to his Maker, and to inflict aggravated social wrong. Into every human being God has breathed an immortal spirit more precious than the whole outward creation. No earthly or celestial language can exaggerate the worth of a human being. No matter how obscure his condition. Thought, Reason, Conscience, the capacity of Virtue, the capacity of Christian Love, an Immortal Destiny, an intimate moral connexion with God, — here are attributes of our common humanity which reduce to insignificance all outward distinctions, and make every human being unspeakably dear to his Maker. No matter how ignorant he may be. The capacity of Improvement allies him to the more instructed of his race, and places within his reach the knowledge and happiness of higher worlds. Every human being has in him the germ of the greatest Idea in the universe, the Idea of God; and to unfold this is the end of his existence. Every human being has in his breast the elements of that Divine, Everlasting Law, which the highest orders of the creation obey. He has the Idea of Duty; and to unfold, revere, obey this is the very purpose for which life was given. Every human being has the Idea of what is meant by that word, Truth; that is, he sees, however dimly, the great object of Divine and created intelligence, and is capable of ever-enlarging perceptions of Truth. Every human being has affections, which may be purified and expanded into a Sublime Love. He has, too, the Idea of Happiness, and a thirst for it which cannot be appeased. Such is our nature. Wherever we see a man, we see the possessor of these great capacities. Did God make such a being to be owned as a tree or a brute? How plainly was he made to exercise, unfold, improve his highest powers, made for a moral, spiritual good! and how is he wronged, and his Creator opposed, when he is forced and broken into a tool to another's physical enjoyment!

Such a being was plainly made for an End in Himself. He is a Person, not a Thing. He is an End, not a mere Instrument or Means. He was made for his own virtue and happiness. Is this end reconcileable with his being held and used as a chattel? The sacrifice of such a being to another's will, to another's present, outward, ill-comprehended good, is the greatest violence which can be offered to any creature of God. It is to degrade him from his rank in the universe, to make him a means, not an end, to cast him out from God's spiritual family into the brutal herd.

Such a being was plainly made to obey a Law within Himself. This is the essence of a moral being. He possesses, as a part of his nature, and the most essential part, a sense of Duty, which he is to reverence and follow, in opposition to all pleasure or pain, to all interfering human wills. The great purpose of all good education and discipline is, to make a man Master of Himself, to excite him to act from a principle in his own mind, to lead him to propose his own perfection as his supreme law and end. And is this highest purpose of man's nature to be reconciled with entire subjection to a foreign will, to an outward, overwhelming force, which is satisfied with nothing but complete submission?

The end of such a being as we have described is manifestly Improvement. Now, it is the fundamental law of our nature, that all our powers are to improve by free exertion. Action is the indispensable condition of progress to the intellect, conscience and heart. Is it not plain, then, that a human being cannot, without wrong, be owned by another, who claims, as proprietor, the right to repress the powers of his slaves, to withold from them the means of devolopement, to keep them within the limits which are necessary to contentment in chains, to shut out every ray of light and every generous sentiment, which may interfere with entire subjection to his will?

No man, who seriously considers what human nature is, and what it was made for, can think of setting up a claim to a fellow-creature. What! own a spiritual being, a being made to know and adore God, and who is to outlive the sun and stars! What! chain to our lowest uses a being made for truth and virtue! Convert into a brute instrument that intelligent nature on which the Idea of Duty has dawned, and which is a nobler type of God than all outward creation! Should we not deem it a wrong which no punishment could expiate, were one of our children seized as property, and driven by the whip to toil? And shall God's child, dearer to him than an only son to a human parent, be thus degraded? Every thing else may be owned in the universe; but a moral, rational being cannot be property. Suns and stars may be owned, but not the lowest spirit. Touch any thing but this. Lay not your hand on God's rational offspring. The whole spiritual world cries out, Forbear! The highest intelligences recognise their own nature, their own rights, in the humblest human being. By that priceless, immortal spirit which dwells in him, by that likeness of God which he wears, tread him not in the dust, confound him not with the brute.

We have thus seen that a human being cannot rightfully be held and used as property. No legislation, not that of all countries or worlds, could make him so. Let this be laid down, as a first, fundamental truth. Let us hold it fast, as a most sacred, precious truth. Let us hold it fast against all customs, all laws, all rank, wealth, and power. Let it be armed with the whole authority of the civilized and Christian world.

I have taken it for granted that no reader would be so wanting in moral discrimination and moral feeling, as to urge that men may rightfully be seized and held as property, because various governments have so ordained. What! is human legislation the measure of right? Are God's laws to be repealed by man's? Can government do no wrong? What is the history of human governments but a record of wrongs? How much does the progress of civilization consist in the substitution of just and humane, for barbarous and oppressive laws? Government, indeed, has ordained slavery and to government the individual is in no case to offer resistance. But criminal legislation ought to be freely and earnestly exposed. Injustice is never so terrible, and never so corrupting, as when armed with the sanctions of law. The authority of government, instead of being a reason for silence under wrongs, is a reason for protesting against wrong with the undivided energy of argument, entreaty, and solemn admonition.

B

CHAPTER II.

RIGHTS.

I NOW proceed to the second division of the subject. I am
to show, that man has by nature received sacred, inalienable
Rights, which are violated by slavery. Some important principles, which belong to this head, were necessarily antici-
pated under the preceding; but they need a fuller exposition.
The whole subject of Rights needs to be considered. Specu-
lations and reasonings about it have lately been given to the
public, not only false, but dangerous to freedom, and there
is a strong tendency to injurious views. Rights are made to
depend on circumstances, so that pretences may easily
be made or created for violating them successively, till none
shall remain. Human rights have been represented as so
modified and circumscribed by men's entrance into the social
state, that only the shadows of them are left. They have
been spoken of as absorbed in the public good; so that a man
may be innocently enslaved, if the public good shall so require. To meet fully all these errors, for such I hold them,
a larger work than the present is required. The nature of
man, his relations to the state, the limits of civil government,
the elements of the public good, and the degree to which the
individual must be surrendered to this good,—these are the
topics which the present subject involves. I cannot enter
into them particularly, but shall lay down what seem to me
the great and true principles in regard to them. I shall show
that man has rights from his very nature, not the gifts of society, but of God; that they are not surrendered on entering
the social state; that they must not be taken away under the
plea of public good; that the Individual is never to be sacrificed to the Community; that the Idea of Rights is to prevail
above all the interests of the state.

Man has rights by nature. The disposition of some to deride abstract rights, as if all rights were uncertain, mutable,
and conceded by society, shows a lamentable ignorance of
human nature. Whoever understands this must see in it an
immovable foundation of rights. These are gifts of the Creator, not grants of society. In the order of things, they precede society, lie at its foundation, constitute man's capacity
for it, and are the great objects of social institutions. The
consciousness of rights is not a creation of human art, a con-
ventional sentiment, but essential to and inseparable from the
human soul.

Man's rights belong to him as a Moral being, as capable of
perceiving moral distinctions, as a subject of moral obligation.
As soon as he becomes conscious of Duty, a kindred consciousness springs up, that he has a Right to do what the sense
of duty enjoins, and that no foreign will or power can obstruct
his moral action without crime. He feels that the sense of
duty was given to him as a Law, that it makes him responsible for himself, that to exercise, unfold, and obey it is the
end of his being, and that he has a right to exercise and obey
it without hindrance or opposition. A consciousness of dignity, however obscure, belongs also to this divine principle;
and though he may want words to do justice to his thoughts,
he feels that he has that within him which makes him essentially equal to all around him.

The sense of duty is the fountain of human rights. In
other words, the same inward principle, which teaches the
former, bears witness to the latter. Duties and Rights must
stand or fall together. It has been too common to oppose
them to one another; but they are indissolubly joined together. That same inward principle, which teaches a man what
he is bound to do to others, teaches equally, and at the same
instant, what others are bound to do to *him*. That same
voice, which forbids him to injure a single fellow-creature,
forbids every fellow-creature to do *him* harm. His conscience,
in revealing the moral law, does not reveal a law for himself
only, but speaks as an Universal Legislator. He has an in-
tuitive conviction, that the obligations of this divine code press
on others as truly as on himself. That principle, which
teaches him that he sustains the relation of brotherhood to all

human beings, teaches him that this relation is reciprocal, that it gives indestructible claims as well as imposes solemn duties, and that what he owes to the members of this vast family, they owe to him in return. Thus the moral nature involves rights. These enter into its very essence. They are taught by the very voice which enjoins duty. Accordingly there is no deeper principle in human nature than the consciousness of rights. So profound, so ineradicable is this sentiment, that the oppressions of ages have no where wholly stifled it.

Having shown the foundation of human rights in human nature, it may be asked what they are. Perhaps they do not admit very accurate definition any more than human duties; for the Spiritual cannot be weighed and measured like the Material. Perhaps a minute criticism may find fault with the most guarded exposition of them; but they may easily be stated in language which the unsophisticated mind will recognise as the truth. Volumes could not do justice to them; and yet perhaps they may be comprehended in one sentence, They may all be comprised in the Right, which belongs to every rational being, to exercise his powers for the promotion of his own and others' Happiness and Virtue. These are the great purposes of his existence. For these his powers were given, and to these he is bound to devote them. He is bound to make himself and others better and happier, according to his ability. His ability for this work is a sacred trust from God, the greatest of all trusts. He must answer for the waste or abuse of it. He consequently suffers an unspeakable wrong, when stripped of it by others, or forbidden to employ it for the end for which it is given; when the powers which God has given for such generous uses are impaired or destroyed by others, or the means for their action and growth are forcibly withheld. As every human being is bound to employ his faculties for his own and others' good, there is an obligation on each to leave all free for the accomplishment of this end; and whoever respects this obligation, whoever uses his own, without invading others' powers, or obstructing others' duties has a sacred, indefeasible right to be unassailed, unobstructed, unharmed by all with whom he may be connected. Here is the grand, all comprehending right of human nature. Every man should revere it, should assert it for himself and for all, and should bear solemn testimony against every infraction of it, by whomsoever made or endured.

Having considered the great fundamental right of human nature, particular rights may easily be deduced. Every man has a right to exercise and invigorate his intellect or the power of knowledge, for knowledge is the essential condition of successful effort for every good ; and whoever obstructs or quenches the intellectual life in another inflicts a grievous and irreparable wrong. Every man has a right to inquire into his duty, and to conform himself to what he learns of it. Every man has a right to use the means, given by God and sanctioned by virtue, for bettering his condition. He has a right to be respected according to his moral worth ; a right to be regarded as a member of the community to which he belongs, and to be protected by impartial laws ; and a right to be exempted from coercion, stripes, and punishment, as long as he respects the rights of others. He has a right to an equivalent for his labor. He has a right to sustain domestic relations, to discharge their duties, and to enjoy the happiness which flows from fidelity in these and other domestic relations. Such are a few of human rights ; and if so, what a grievous wrong is slavery !

Perhaps nothing has done more to impair the sense of the reality and sacredness of human rights, and to sanction oppression, than loose ideas as to the change made in man's natural rights by his entrance into civil society. It is commonly said that men part with a portion of these by becoming a community, a body politic ; that government consists of powers surrendered by the individual ; and it is said, " If certain rights and powers may be surrendered, why not others ? why not all ? What limit is to be set ? The good of the community, to which a part is given up, may demand the whole ; and in this good, all private rights are merged." This is the logic of despotism. We are grieved, that it finds its way into republics, and that it sets down the great principles of freedom as abstractions and metaphysical theories, good enough for the cloister, but too refined for practical and real life.

Human rights, however, are not to be so reasoned away. They belong, as we have seen, to man as a moral being, and

B 3

nothing can divest him of them but the destruction of his nature. They are not to be given up to society as a prey. On the contrary, the great end of civil society is to secure them. The great end of government is to repress *all wrong.* Its highest function is to protect the weak against the powerful, so that the obscurest human being may enjoy his rights in peace. Strange that an institution, built on the idea of Rights, should be used to unsettle this idea, to confuse our moral perceptions, to sanctify wrongs as means of general good.

It is said that in forming civil society the individual surrenders a part of his rights. It would be more proper to say that he adopts new modes of securing them. He consents, for example, to desist from self-defence, that he and all may be more effectually defended by the public force. He consents to submit his cause to an umpire or tribunal, that justice may be more impartially awarded, and that he and all may more certainly receive their due. He consents to part with a portion of his property in taxation, that his own and others' property may be the more secure. He submits to certain restraints, that he and others may enjoy more enduring freedom. He expects an equivalent for what he relinquishes, and insists on it as his right. He is wronged by partial laws, which compel him to contribute to the state beyond his proportion, his ability, and the measure of benefits he receives. How absurd is it to suppose, that by consenting to be protected by the state, and by yielding it the means, he surrenders the very rights which were the objects of his accession to the social compact !

The authority of the state to impose laws on its members I cheerfully allow ; but this has limits, which are found to be more and more narrow in proportion to the progress of moral science. The state is equally restrained with individuals by the moral law. For example, it may not, must not on any account, put an innocent man to death, or require of him a dishonorable or criminal service. It may demand allegiance, but only on the ground of the protection it affords. It may levy taxes, but only because it takes all property and all interests under its shield. It may pass laws, but only impartial ones, framed for the whole and not for the few. It must not seize by a special act the property of the humblest individual, without making him an equivalent. It must regard every man, over whom it extends its authority, as a vital part of itself, as entitled to its care and to its provisions for liberty and happiness. If, in an emergency, its safety, which is the interest of each and all, may demand the imposition of peculiar restraints on one or many, it is bound to limit these restrictions to the precise point which its safety prescribes, to remove the necessity of them as far and as fast as possible, to compensate by peculiar protection such as it deprives of the ordinary means of protecting themselves, and, in general, to respect and provide for liberty in the very acts which for a time restrain it. The idea of Rights, I repeat it, should be fundamental and supreme in civil institutions. Government becomes a nuisance and scourge, in proportion as it sacrifices these to the many or the few. Government, I repeat it, is equally bound with the individual by the moral law. The ideas of Justice and Rectitude, of what is due to man from his fellow-creatures, of the claims of every moral being, are far deeper and more primitive than Civil Polity. Government, far from originating them, owes to them its strength. Right is older than human law. Law ought to be its voice. It should be built on and should correspond to the principle of justice in the human breast, and its weakness is owing to nothing more than to its clashing with our indestructible moral convictions.

That government is most perfect, in which Policy is most entirely subjected to Justice, or in which the supreme and constant aim is to secure the rights of every human being. This is the beautiful idea of a free government, and no government is free but in proportion as it realizes this. Liberty must not be confounded with popular institutions. A representative government may be as despotic as an absolute monarchy. In as far as it tramples on the rights, whether of many or one, it is a despotism. The sovereign power, whether wielded by a single hand or several hands, by a king or a congress, which spoils one human being of the immunities and privileges bestowed on him by God, is so far a tyranny. The great argument in favor of representative institutions is, that a people's rights are safest in their own hands, and should never be surrendered to an irresponsible power. Rights, lie at the foundation of a popular government; and when this betrays them, the wrong is more aggravated than when they are crushed by despotism.

Still the question will be asked, " Is not the General Good the supreme, law of the state? Are not all restraints on the individual just, which this demands? When the rights of the individual clash with this, must they not yield? Do they not, indeed, cease to be rights? Must not every thing give place to the General Good? I have started this question in various forms, because I deem it worthy of particular examination. Public and private morality, the freedom and safety of our national institutions, are greatly concerned in setting the claims of the " General Good." In monarchies, the Divine Right of kings swallowed up all others. In republics the General Good threatens the same evil. It is a shelter for the abuses and usurpations of government, for the profligacies of states-men, for the vices of parties, for the wrongs of slavery. In considering this subject, I take the hazard of repeating princi-ples already laid down; but this will be justified by the impor-tance of reaching and determining the truth. Is the General Good, then, the supreme law to which every thing must bow?

This question may be settled at once by proposing another. Suppose the Public Good to require that a number of the members of a state, no matter how few, should perjure them-selves, or should disclaim their faith in God and virtue. Would their right to follow conscience and God be annulled? Would they be bound to sin? Suppose a conqueror to menace a state with ruin, unless its members should insult their parents, and stain themselves with crimes at which nature revolts? Must the Public Good prevail over purity and our holiest affections? Do we not all feel, that there are higher goods than even the safety of the state? That there is a higher law than that of mightiest empires? That the idea of Rectitude is deeper in human nature than that of private or public interest? And that this is to bear sway over all private and public acts?

The supreme law of a state is not its safety, its power, its prosperity, its affluence, the flourishing state of agriculture, commerce, and the arts. These objects, constituting what is commonly called the Public Good, are, indeed, proposed, and ought to be proposed, in the constitution and administration of states. But there is a higher law, even Virtue, Rectitude, the Voice of Conscience, the Will of God. Justice is a greater good than property, not greater in degree, but in kind. Universal benevolence is infinitely superior to prosperity. Religion, the love of God, is worth incomparably more than all his outward gifts. A community, to secure or aggrandize itself, must never forsake the Right, the Holy, the Just.

Moral Good, Rectitude, in all its branches, is the Supreme Good; by which I do not intend that it is the surest means to the security and prosperity of the state. Such, indeed, it is, but this is too low a view. It must not be looked upon as a Means, an Instrument. It is the Supreme End, and states are bound to subject to it all their legislation, be the apparent loss of prosperity ever so great. National wealth is not the End. It derives all its worth from national virtue. If accumulated by rapacity, conquest, or any degrading means, or if concentrated in the hands of the few, whom it strengthens to crush the many, it is a curse. National wealth is a blessing, only when it springs from and represents the intelligence and virtue of the community, when it is a fruit and expression of good habits, of respect for the rights of all, of impartial and beneficent legislation, when it gives impulse to the higher faculties, and occasion and incitement to justice and benefi- cence. No greater calamity can befall a people than to pros- per by crime. No success can be a compensation for the wound inflicted on a nation's mind by renouncing Right as its Supreme Law.

Let a people exalt Prosperity above Rectitude, and a more dangerous end cannot be proposed. Public Prosperity, Gene- ral Good, regarded by itself, or apart from the moral law, is something vague, unsettled, and uncertain, and will infallibly be so construed by the selfish and grasping as to secure their own aggrandizement. It may be made to wear a thousand forms according to men's interests and passions. This is illustrated by every day's history. Not a party springs up, which does not sanctify all its projects for monopolizing power by the plea of General Good. Not a measure, however ruin- ous, can be proposed, which cannot be shown to favor one or another national interest. The truth is, that, in the uncer- tainty of human affairs, an uncertainty growing out of the infinite and very subtile causes which are acting on communities, the consequences of no measure can be foretold with certainty. The best concerted schemes of policy often fail; whilst a rash and profligate administration may, by unexpected concurrences of events, seem to advance a nation's glory. In regard to the means of national prosperity the wisest are weak judges. For example, the present rapid growth of this country, carrying, as it does, vast multitudes beyond the institutions of religion and education, may be working ruin, whilst the people exult in it as a pledge of greatness. We are too short-sighted to find our law in outward interests. To states, as to individuals, Rectitude is the Supreme Law. It was never designed that the Public Good, as disjoined from this, as distinct from justice and reverence for all rights, should be comprehended and made our end. Statesmen work in the dark, until the idea of Right towers above expediency or wealth. Woe to that people which would found its prosperity in wrong! It is time that the low maxims of policy, which have ruled for ages, should fall. It is time that Public Interest should no longer hallow injustice, and fortify government in making the weak their prey.

In this discussion, I have used the phrase, Public or General Good, in its common acceptation, as signifying the safety and prosperity of a state. Why can it not be used in a larger sense? Why can it not be made to comprehend inward and moral, as well as outward good? And why cannot the former be understood to be incomparably the most important element of the public weal? Then, indeed, I should assent to the proposition, that the General Good is the supreme law. So construed, it would support the great truths which I have maintained. It would condemn the infliction of wrong on the humblest individual, as a national calamity. It would plead with us to extend to every individual the means of improving his character and lot.

If the remarks under this head be just, it will follow that the good of the Individual is more important than the outward prosperity of the State. The former is not vague and unsettled, like the latter, and it belongs to a higher order of interests. It consists of the free exertion and expansion of the individual's powers, especially of his higher faculties; in the energy of his intellect, conscience, and good affections; in sound judgment; in the acquisition of truth; in laboring honestly for himself and his family; in loving his Creator, and subjecting his own will to the Divine; in loving his fellow-creatures, and making cheerful sacrifices to their happiness; in friendship; in sensibility to the beautiful, whether in nature or art; in loyalty to his principles; in moral courage; in self-respect; in understanding and asserting his rights; and in the Christian hope of immortality. Such is the good of the Individual; a more sacred, exalted, enduring interest, than any accessions of wealth or power to the State. Let it not be sacrificed to these. He should find, in his connexions with the community, aids to the accomplishment of these purposes of his being, and not be chained and subdued by it to the inferior interests of any fellow-creature.

In all ages the Individual has in one form or another been trodden in the dust. In monarchies and aristocracies he has been sacrificed to One or to the Few; who, regarding government as an heir-loom in their families, and thinking of the people as made only to live and die for their glory, have not dreamed that the sovereign power was designed to shield every man, without exception, from wrong. In the ancient Republics, the Glory of the State, especially Conquest, was the end to which the individual was expected to offer himself a victim, and in promoting which no cruelty was to be declined, no human right revered. He was merged in a great whole, called the Commonwealth, to which his whole nature was to be immolated. It was the glory of the American people, that in their Declaration of Independance they took the ground of the indestructible rights of every human being. They declared all men to be essentially equal, and each born to be free. They did not, like the Greek or Roman, assert for themselves liberty, which they burned to wrest from other states. They spoke in the name of humanity, as the representatives of the rights of the feeblest, as well as mightiest, of their race. They published universal, everlasting principles, which are to work out the deliverance of every human being. Such was their glory. Let not the idea of Rights be eraced from their children's minds by false ideas of public good. Let not the sacredness of individual man be forgotten in the feverish pursuit of property. It is more important that the Individual should respect himself, and be respected by others, than that the wealth of both worlds should be accumulated on our shores. National wealth is not the end of society. It may exist where large classes are depressed and wronged. It may undermine a nation's spirit, institutions, and independence. It can have no value and no sure foundation, until the Supremacy of the Rights of the Individual is the first article of a nation's faith, and until reverence for them becomes the spirit of public men.

Perhaps it will be replied to all which has now been said, that there is an argument from experience, which invalidates the doctrines of this section. It may be said, that human rights, notwithstanding what has been said of their sacredness, do and must yield to the exigencies of real life, that there is often a stern necessity in human affairs to which they bow. I may be asked, whether, in the history of nations, circumstances do not occur, in which the rigor of the principles, now laid down, must be relaxed? Whether, in seasons of imminent peril to the state, private rights must not give way? I may be asked, whether the establishment of martial law and a dictator has not sometimes been justified and demanded by public danger, and whether, of course, the rights and liberties of the individual are not held at the discretion of the state. I admit, in reply, that extreme cases may occur, in which the exercise of rights and freedom may be suspended; but suspended only for their ultimate and permanent security. At such times, when the frantic fury of the many, or the usurpations of the few interrupt the administration of law, and menace property and life, society, threatened with ruin, puts forth instinctively spasmodic efforts for its own preservation. It flies to an irresponsible director for its protection. But in these cases, the great idea of Rights predominates amidst their apparent subversion. A power above all laws is conferred, only that the empire of law may be restored. Despotic restraints are imposed only that liberty may be rescued from ruin. All rights are involved in the safety of the state; and hence, in the cases referred to, the safety of the state becomes the supreme law. The individual is bound for a time to forego his freedom for the salvation of institutions, without which liberty is but a name. To argue from such sacrifices that he may be permanently made a slave, is as great an insult to reason as to humanity. It may be added, that sacrifices, which may be demanded for the safety, are not due from the individual to the prosperity of the state. The great end of civil society is to secure rights, not accumulate wealth; and to merge the former in the latter is to turn political union into degradation and a scourge. The community is bound to take the rights of each and all under its guardianship. It must substantiate its claim to universal obedience by redeeming its pledge of universal protection. It must immolate no man to the prosperity of the rest. Its laws should be made for all, its tribunals opened to all. It cannot without guilt abandon any of its members to private oppression, to irresponsible power.

We have thus established the reality and sacredness of human rights; and that slavery is an infraction of these is too plain to need any labored proof. Slavery violates not one, but all; and violates them not incidentally, but necessarily, systematically, from its very nature. In starting with the assumption that the slave is property, it sweeps away every defence of human rights and lays them in the dust. Were it necessary I might enumerate them, and show how all fall before this terrible usurpation; but a few remarks will suffice.

Slavery strips man of the fundamental right to inquire into, consult, and seek his own happiness. His powers belong to another, and for another they must be used. He must form no plans, engage in no enterprises, for bettering his condition. Whatever be his capacities, however equal to great improvements of his lot, he is chained for life by another's will to the same unvaried toil. He is forbidden to do for himself or others the work, for which God stamped him with his own image, and endowed him with his own best gifts.—Again, the slave is stripped of the right to acquire property. Being himself owned, his earnings belong to another. He can possess nothing but by favor. That right on which the developement of men's powers so much depends, the right to make accumulations, to gain exclusive possessions by honest industry, is witheld. "The slave can acquire nothing," says one of the slave-codes, "but what must belong to his master;" and however this definition, which moves the indignation of the free, may be mitigated by favor, the spirit of it enters into the very essence of slavery.—Again, the slave is stripped of his right to his wife and children. They belong to another and may be torn from him, one and all, at any moment, at his master's pleasure. — Again, the slave is stripped of the right to the culture of his rational powers. He is in some cases deprived by law of instruction, which is placed within his reach by the improvements of society and the philanthropy of the age. He is not allowed to toil, that his children may enjoy a better education than himself. The most sacred right of human nature, that of developing his best faculties, is denied. Even should it be granted, it would be conceded as a favor, and might at any moment be withheld by the capricious will of another.—Again, the slave is deprived of the right of self-defence. No injury from a white man is he suffered to repel, nor can he seek redress from the laws of his country. If accumulated insult and wrong provoke him to the slightest retaliation, this effort for self-protection, allowed and commended to others, is a crime for which he must pay a fearful penalty.—Again, the slave is stripped of the right to be exempted from all harm except for wrong doing. He is subjected to the lash, by those whom he has never consented to serve, and whose claim to him as property we have seen to be a usurpation; and this power of punishment, which, if justly claimed, should be exercised with a fearful care, is often delegated to men in whose hands there is a moral certainty of its abuse.

I will add but one more example of the violation of human rights by slavery. The slave virtually suffers the wrong of robbery, though with utter unconsciousness on the part of those who inflict it. It may, indeed, be generally thought, that, as he is suffered to own nothing, he cannot fall, at least, under this kind of violence. But it is not true that he owns nothing. Whatever he may be denied by man, he holds from nature the most valuable property, and that from which all other is derived, I mean his strength. His labor is his own, by the gift of that God who nerved his arm, and gave him intelligence and conscience to direct the use of it for his own and other's happiness. No possession is so precious as a man's force of body and mind. The exertion of this in labor is the great foundation and source of property in outward things. The worth of articles of traffic is measured by the labor expended in their production. To the great mass of men, in all countries, their strength or labor is their whole fortune. To seize on this would be to rob them of their all. In truth, no robbery is so great as that to which the slave is habitually subjected. To take by force a man's whole estate, the fruit of years of toil, would by universal consent be denounced as a great wrong; but what is this, compared with seizing the man himself, and appropriating to our use the limbs, faculties, strength, and labor, by which all property is won and held fast? The right of property in outward things is as nothing, compared with our right to ourselves. Were the slave-holder stript of his fortune, he would count the violence slight, compared with what he would suffer, were his person seized and devoted as a chattel to another's use. Let it not be said that the slave receives an equivalent, that he is fed and clothed, and is not, therefore, robbed. Suppose another to wrest from us a valued possession, and to pay us his own price. Should we not think ourselves robbed? Would not the laws pronounce the invader a robber? Is it consistent with the right of property, that a man should determine the equivalent for what he takes from his neighbour? Especially is it to be hoped, that the equivalent due to the laborer will be scrupulously weighed, when he himself is held as property, and all his earnings are declared to be his master's? So great an infraction of human right is slavery!

In reply to these remarks, it may be said that the theory and practice of slavery differ; that the rights of the slave are not as wantonly sported with as the claims of the master might lead us to infer; that some of his possessions are sacred; that not a few slave-holders refuse to divorce husband and wife, to sever parent and child; and that in many cases the power of punishment is used so reluctantly, as to encourage insolence and insubordination. All this I have no disposition to deny. Indeed it must be so. It is not in human nature to wink wholly out of sight the rights of a fellow-creature. Degrade him as we may, we cannot altogether forget his claims. In every slave country, there are, undoubtedly, masters who desire and purpose to respect these, to the full extent which the nature of the relation will allow. Still, human rights are denied. They lie wholly at another's mercy; and we must have studied history in vain, if we need be told that they will be continually the prey of this absolute power.—The Evils involved in and flowing from the denial and infraction of the rights of the slave will form the subject of a subsequent chapter.

CHAPTER III.

―

EXPLANATIONS.

I HAVE endeavoured to show in the preceding sections that
slavery is a violation of sacred rights, the infliction of a great
wrong. And here a question arises. It may be asked, whether, by this language, I intend to fasten on the slave-holder
the charge of a peculiar guilt. On this point great explicit-
ness is a duty. Sympathy with the slave is often degenerated
into injustice towards the master. I wish it, then, to be understood, that, in ranking slavery among the greatest wrongs,
I speak of the injury endured by the slave, and not of the
character of the master. These are distinct points. The former does not determine the latter. The wrong is the same to
the slave, from whatever motive or spirit it may be inflicted.
But this motive or spirit determines wholly the character of
him who inflicts it. Because a great injury is done to another, it does not follow that he who does it is a depraved man;
for he may do it unconsciously, and, still more, may do it in
the belief that he confers a good. We have learned little of
moral science and of human nature, if we do not know that
guilt is to be measured, not by the outward act, but by unfaithfulness to conscience; and that the consciences of men
are often darkened by education, and other inauspicious influences. All men have partial consciences, or want comprehension of some duties. All partake, in a measure, of the
errors of the community in which they live. Some are be-
trayed into moral mistakes by the very force with which
conscience acts in regard to some particular duty. As the
intellect, in grasping one truth, often loses its hold of others,
and by giving itself up to one idea, falls into exaggeration;
so the moral sense, in seizing on a particular exercise of philanthropy, forgets other duties, and will even violate many
important precepts in its passionate eagerness to carry one to

perfection. Innumerable illustrations may be given of the liableness of men to moral error. The practice, which strikes one man with horror, may seem to another, who was born and brought up in the midst of it, not only innocent, but meritorious. We must judge others, not by our light, but by their own. We must take their place, and consider what allowance we in their position might justly expect. Our ancestors at the North were concerned in the slave-trade. Some of us can recollect individuals of the colored race, who were torn from Africa, and grew old under our parental roofs. Our ancestors committed a deed now branded as piracy. Were they, therefore, the offscouring of the earth? Were not some of them among the best of their times? The administration of religion in almost all past ages has been a violation of the sacred rights of conscience. How may sects have persecuted and shed blood! Were their members, therefore, monsters of depravity? The history of our race is made up of wrongs, many of which were committed without a suspicion of their true character, and many from an urgent sense of duty. A man born among slaves, accustomed to this relation from his birth, taught its necessity by venerated parents, associating it with all whom he reveres, and too familiar with its evils to see and feel their magnitude, can hardly be expected to look on slavery as it appears to more impartial and distant observers. Let it not be said that when new light is offered him he is criminal in rejecting it. Are we all willing to receive new light? Can we wonder that such a man should be slow to be convinced of the criminality of an abuse sanctioned by prescription, and which has so interwoven itself with all the habits, employments, and economy of life, that he can hardly conceive of the existence of society without this all-pervading element? May he not be true to his convictions of duty in other relations, though he grievously err in this? If, indeed, through cupidity and selfishness, he stifle the monitions of conscience, warp his judgment, and repel the light, he incurs great guilt. If he want virtue to resolve on doing right, though at the loss of every slave, he incurs great guilt. But who of us can look into his heart? To whom are the secret workings there revealed?

Still more. There are masters who have thrown off the

natural prejudices of their position, who see slavery as it is, and who hold the slave chiefly, if not wholly, from disinterested considerations; and these deserve great praise. They deplore and abhor the institution; but believing that partial emancipation, in the present condition of society, would bring unmixed evil on bond and free, they think themselves bound to continue the relation, until it shall be dissolved by comprehensive and systematic measures of the state. There are many of them who would shudder as much as we at reducing a freeman to bondage, but who are appalled by what seem to them the perils and difficulties of liberating multitudes, born and brought up to that condition. There are many, who, nominally holding the slave as property, still hold him for his own good and for the public order, and would blush to retain him on other grounds. Are such men to be set down among the unprincipled? Am I told that by these remarks I extenuate slavery? I reply, slavery is still a heavy yoke, and strips man of his dearest rights, be the master's character what it may. Slavery is not less a curse, because long use may have blinded most, who support it, to its evils. Its influence is still blighting, though conscientiously upheld. Absolute monarchy is still a scourge, though among despots there have been good men. It is possible to abhor and oppose bad institutions, and yet to abstain from indiscriminate condemnation of those who cling to them, and even to see in their ranks greater virtue than in ourselves. It is true, and ought to be cheerfully acknowledged, that in the slave-holding States may be found some of the greatest names of our history, and, what is still more important, bright examples of private virtue and Christian love.

There is, however, there must be, in slave-holding communities a large class which cannot be too severely condemned. There are many, we fear, very many, who hold their fellow-creatures in bondage, from selfish, base motives. They hold the slave for gain, whether justly or unjustly they neither ask nor care. They cling to him as property, and have no faith in the principles which will diminish a man's wealth. They hold him, not for his own good or the safety of the state, but with precisely the same views with which they hold a laboring horse, that is, for the profit which they wring from him. They will not hear a word of his wrongs; for, wronged or not, they will not let him go. He is their property, and they mean not to be poor for righteousness' sake. Such a class there undoubtedly is among slave-holders; how large their own consciences must determine. We are sure of it; for under such circumstances human nature will and must come to this mournful result. Now, to men of this spirit, the explanations we have made do in no degree apply. Such men ought to tremble before the rebukes of outraged humanity and indignant virtue. Slavery, upheld for gain, is a great crime. He, who has nothing to urge against emancipation, but that it will make him poorer, is bound to Immediate Emancipation. He has no excuse for wresting from his brethren their rights. The plea of benefit to the slave and the state avails him nothing. He extorts, by the lash, that labor to which he has no claim, through a base selfishness. Every morsel of food, thus forced from the injured, ought to be bitterer than gall. His gold is cankered. The sweat of the slave taints the luxuries for which it streams. Better were it for the selfish wrong doer of whom I speak, to live as the slave, to clothe himself in the slave's raiment, to eat the slave's coarse food, to till his fields with his own hands, than to pamper himself by day, and pillow his head on down at night, at the cost of a wantonly injured fellow-creature. No fellow-creature can be so injured without taking terrible vengeance. He is terribly avenged even now. The blight which falls on the soul of the wrong doer, the desolation of his moral nature, is a more terrible calamity than he inflicts. In deadening his moral feeling, he dies to the proper happiness of a man. In hardening his heart against his fellow-creatures, he sears it to all true joy. In shutting his ear against the voice of justice, he shuts out all the harmonies of the universe, and turns the voice of God within him into rebuke. He may prosper, indeed, and hold faster the slave by whom he prospers; but he rivets heavier and more ignominious chains on his own soul than he lays on others. No punishment is so terrible as prosperous guilt. No fiend, exhausting on us all his power of torture, is so terrible as an oppressed fellow-creature. The cry of the oppressed, unheard on earth, is heard in heaven. God is just, and if justice reign, then the unjust must terribly suffer. Then no being can profit by evil doing. Then all the laws of the universe are ordinances against guilt. Then every enjoyment, gained by wrong doing, will be turned into a curse. No laws of nature are so irrepealable as that law which binds guilt and misery. God is just. Then all the defences, which the oppressor rears against the consequences of wrong doing, are vain, as vain as would be his strivings to arrest by his single arm the ocean or whirlwind. He may disarm the slave. Can he disarm that slave's Creator? He can crush the spirit of insurrection in a fellow-creature. Can he crush the awful spirit of justice and retribution in the Almighty? He can still the murmur of discontent in his victim. Can he silence that voice which speaks in thunder, and is to break the sleep of the grave? Can he always still the reproving, avenging voice in his own breast?

I know it will be said, "You would make us poor." Be poor, then, and thank God for your honest poverty. Better be poor than unjust. Better beg than steal. Better live in an alms-house, better die, than trample on a fellow-creature and reduce him to a brute, for selfish gratification. What! Have we yet to learn that "it profits us nothing to gain the whole world, and lose our souls?"

Let it not be replied, in scorn, that we of the North, notorious for love of money, and given to selfish calculations, are not the people to call others to resign their wealth. I have no desire to shield the North. We have, without doubt, a great multitude, who, were they slave-holders, would sooner die than relax their iron grasp, than yield their property in men to justice and the commands of God. We have those who would fight against abolition, if by this measure the profit of their intercourse with the South should be materially impaired. The present excitement among us is, in part, the working of mercenary principles. But because the North joins hands with the South, shall iniquity go unpunished or unrebuked? Can the league of the wicked, the revolt of worlds, repeal the everlasting law of heaven and earth? Has God's throne fallen before Mammon's? Must duty find no voice, no organ, because corruption is universally diffused? Is not this a fresh motive to solemn warning, that, every where, Northward and Southward, the rights of human beings are held so cheap, in comparison with worldly gain?

CHAPTER IV.

THE EVILS OF SLAVERY.

THE subject of this section is painful and repulsive. We must not, however, turn away from the contemplation of human sufferings and guilt. Evil is permitted by the Creator, that we should strive against it in faith, and hope, and charity. We must never quail before it because of its extent and duration, never feel as if its power were greater than that of goodness. It is meant to call forth deep sympathy with human nature, and unwearied sacrifices for human redemption. One great part of the mission of every man on earth is to contend with evil in some of its forms; and there are some evils so dependent on opinion, that every man, in judging and reproving them faithfully, does something towards their removal. Let us not, then, shrink from the contemplation of human sufferings. Even sympathy, if we have nothing more to offer, is a tribute acceptable to the Universal Father.—On this topic exaggeration should be conscientiously shunned; and, at the same time, humanity requires that the whole truth should be honestly spoken.

In treating of the evils of slavery, I, of course, speak of its general, not universal effects, of its natural tendencies, not unfailing results. There are the same natural differences among the bond as the free, and there is a great diversity in the circumstances in which they are placed. The house-slave, selected for ability and faithfulness, placed amidst the habits, accommodations, and improvements of civilized life, admitted to a degree of confidence and familiarity, and requiting these privileges with attachment, is almost necessarily more enlightened and respectable than the field-slave, who is confined to monotonous toils, and to the society and influences of beings as degraded as himself. The mechanics in this class are sensibly benefited by occupations which give a higher action to

c 3

the mind. Among the bond, as the free, will be found those to whom nature seems partial, and who are carried almost instinctively towards what is good. I speak of the natural, general influences of slavery. Here, as every where else, there are exceptions to the rule, and exceptions which multiply with the moral improvements of the community in which the slave is found. But these do not determine the general character of the institution. It has general tendencies founded in its very nature, and which predominate vastly wherever it exists. These tendencies it is my present purpose to unfold.

1. The first rank among the evils of slavery must be given to its Moral influence. This is throughout debasing. Common language teaches this. We can say nothing more insulting of another, than that he is slavish. To possess the spirit of a slave is to have sunk to the lowest depths. We can apply to slavery no worse name than its own. Men have always shrunk instinctively from this state, as the most degraded. No punishment, save death, has been more dreaded, and to avoid it death has often been endured.

In expressing the moral influence of slavery the first and most obvious remark is, that it destroys the proper consciousness and spirit of a Man. The slave regarded and treated as property, bought and sold like a brute, denied the rights of humanity, unprotected against insult, made a tool, and systematically subdued, that he may be a manageable, useful tool, how can he help regarding himself as fallen below his race? How must his spirit be crushed! How can he respect himself? He becomes bound to Servility. This word, borrowed from his condition, expresses the ruin wrought by slavery within him. The idea, that he was made for his own virtue and happiness, scarcely dawns on his mind. To be an instrument of the physical, material good of another, whose will is his highest law, he is taught to regard as the great purpose of his being. Here lies the evil of slavery. Its whips, imprisonments, and even the horrors of the middle passage from Africa to America, these are not to be named, in comparison with this extinction of the proper consciousness of a human being, with the degradation of a man into a brute.

It may be said, that the slave is used to his yoke; that his sensibilities are blunted; that he receives, without a pang or a thought, the treatment which would sting other men to madness. And to what does this apology amount? It virtually declares, that slavery has done its perfect work, has quenched the spirit of humanity, that the Man is dead within the Slave. Is slavery, therefore, no wrong? It is not, however, true, that this work of debasement is ever so effectually done as to extinguish all feeling. Man is too great a creature to be wholly ruined by man. When he seems dead he only sleeps. There are occasionally some sullen murmurs in the calm of slavery, showing that life still beats in the soul, that the idea of Rights cannot be wholly effaced from the human being.

It would be too painful, and it is not needed, to detail the processes by which the spirit is broken in slavery. I refer to one only, the selling of slaves. The practice of exposing fellow-creatures for sale, of having markets for men as for cattle, of examining the limbs and muscles of a man and a woman as of a brute, of putting human beings under the hammer of an auctioneer, and delivering them, like any other articles of merchandise, to the highest bidder, all this is such an insult to our common nature, and so infinitely degrading to the poor victim, that it is hard to conceive of its existence, except in a barbarous country.

That slavery should be most unpropitious to the slave as a moral being will be farther apparent, if we consider that his condition is throughout a Wrong, and that consequently it must tend to unsettle all his notions of duty. The violation of his own rights, to which he is inured from birth, must throw confusion over his ideas of all human rights. He cannot comprehend them; or, if he does, how can he respect them, seeing them, as he does, perpetually trampled on in his own person? The injury to the character from living in an atmosphere of wrong, we can all understand. To live in a state of society, of which injustice is the chief and all-pervading element, is too severe a trial for human nature, especially when no means are used to counteract its influence.

Accordingly the most common distinctions of morality are faintly apprehended by the slave. Respect for property, that fundamental law of civil society, can hardly be instilled into him. His dishonesty is proverbial. Theft from his master passes with him for no crime. A system of force is generally found to drive to fraud. How necessarily will this be the result of a relation, in which force is used to extort from a man his labor, his natural property, without an attempt to win his consent! Can we wonder that the uneducated conscience of the man who is daily wronged should allow him in reprisals to the extent of his power? Thus the primary social virtue, justice, is undermined in the slave.

That the slave should yield himself up to intemperance licentiousness, and, in general, to sensual excess, we must also expect. Doomed to live for the physical indulgences of others, unused to any pleasures but those of sense, stripped of self-respect, and having nothing to gain in life, how can he be expected to govern himself? How naturally, I had almost said necessarily, does he become the creature of sensation, of passion, of the present moment! What aid does the future give him in withstanding desire? That better condition, for which other men postpone the cravings of appetite, never opens before him. The sense of character, the power of opinion, another restraint on the free, can do little or nothing to rescue so abject a class from excess and debasement. In truth, power over himself is the last virtue we should expect in the slave, when we think of him as subjected to absolute power, and made to move passively from the impulse of a foreign will. He is trained to cowardice, and cowardice links itself naturally with low vices. Idleness to his apprehension is paradise, for he works without hope of reward. Thus slavery robs him of moral force, and prepares him to fall a prey to appetite and passion.

That the slave finds in his condition little nutriment for the social virtues we shall easily understand, if we consider that his chief relations are to an absolute master, and to the companions of his degrading bondage, that is, to a being who wrongs him, and to associates whom he cannot honor, whom he sees debased. His dependence on his owner loosens his ties to all other beings. He has no country to love, no family to call his own, no objects of public utility to espouse, no impulse to generous exertion. The relations, dependencies, and responsibilities, by which Providence forms the soul to a deep, disinterested love, are almost struck out of his lot. An arbitary rule, a foreign, irresistible will, taking him out of his own hands, and placing him beyond the natural influences of society, extinguishes in a great degree the sense of what is due to himself, and to the human family around him.

The effects of slavery on the character are so various, that this part of the discussion might be greatly extended; but I will touch only on one topic. Let us turn, for a moment, to the great Motive by which the slave is made to labor. Labor, in one form or another, is appointed by God for man's improvement and happiness, and absorbs the chief part of human life, so that the Motive which excites to it has immense influence on character. It determines very much, whether life shall serve or fail of its end. The man, who works from honorable motives, from domestic affections, from desire of a condition which will open to him greater happiness and usefulness, finds in labor an exercise and invigoration of virtue. The day-laborer, who earns, with horny hand and the sweat of his face, coarse food for a wife and children whom he loves, is raised, by this generous motive, to true dignity ; and, though wanting the refinements of life, is a nobler being than those who think themselves absolved by wealth from serving others. Now the slave's labor brings no dignity, is an exercise of no virtue, but throughout a degradation; so ˙that one of God's chief provisions for human improvement becomes a curse. The motive from which he acts debases him. It is the Whip. It is corporal punishment. It is physical pain inflicted by a fellow-creature. Undoubtedly labor is mitigated to the slave, as to all men, by habit. But this is not the motive. Take away the Whip, and he would be idle. His labor brings no new comforts to wife or child. The motive which spurs him is one by which it is base to be swayed. Stripes are, indeed, resorted to by civil government, when no other consideration will deter from crime ; but he who is deterred from wrong doing by the whipping-post, is among the most fallen of his race. To work in sight of the whip, under menace of blows, is to be exposed to perpetual insult and degrading influences. Every motion of the limbs, which such a menace urges is a wound to the soul. How hard must it be for a man who lives

under the lash to respect himself! When this motive is sub-
stituted for all the nobler ones which God ordains, is it not
almost necessarily death to the better and higher sentiments
of our nature? It is the part of a man to despise pain, in
comparison with disgrace, to meet it fearlessly in well doing,
to perform the work of life from other impulses. It is the
part of a brute to be governed by the whip. Even the brute
is seen to act from more generous incitements. The horse of
a noble breed will not endure the lash. Shall we sink man
below the horse?

Let it not be said that blows are seldom inflicted. Be it
so. We are glad to know it. But this is not the point. The
complaint now urged is not of the amount of the pain inflicted,
but of its influence on the character when made the great motive to human labor. It is not the endurance, but the dread
of the whip, it is the substitution of this for natural and honorable motives to action, which we abhor and condemn. It
matters not whether few or many are whipped. A blow given
to a single slave is a stripe on the souls of all who see or hear
it. It makes all abject, servile. It is not of the wound given
to the flesh of which we now complain. Scar the back, and
you have done nothing, compared with the wrong done to the
soul. You have either stung that soul with infernal passions,
with thirst for revenge; or, what perhaps is more discourag-
ing, you have broken and brutalized it. The human spirit
has perished under your hands, as far as it can be destroyed
by human force.

I know it is sometimes said, in reply to these remarks, that
all men, as well as slaves, act from necessity; that we have
masters in hunger and thirst; that no man loves labor for
itself; that the pains which are inflicted on us by the laws of
nature, the elements, and seasons, are so many lashes driving
us to our daily task. Be it so. Still the two cases are essentially different. The necessity laid on us by natural wants is
most kindly in its purpose. It is meant to awaken all our
faculties, to give a full play to body and mind, and thus to
give us a new consciousness of the powers derived to us from
God. We are, indeed, subjected to a stern nature; we are
placed amidst warring elements, scorching heat, withering
cold, storms, blights, sickness, death. And what is the design?

To call forth our powers, to lay on us great duties, to make us nobler beings. We are placed in the midst of a warring nature, not to yield to it, not to be its slaves, but to conquer it, to make it the monument of our skill and strength, to arm ourselves with its elements, its heat, winds, vapors, and mineral treasures, to find, in its painful changes, occasions and incitements to invention, courage, endurance, mutual and endearing dependencies, and religious trust. The development of human nature, in all its powers and affections, is the end of that hard necessity which is laid on us by nature. Is this one and the same thing with the whip laid on the slave? Still more; it is the design of nature that by energy, skill, and self-denial we should so far anticipate our wants or accumulate supplies, as to be able to diminish the toil of the hands, and to mix with it more intellectual and liberal occupations. Nature does not lay on us an unchangeable task, but one which we may all lighten by honest, self-denying industry. Thus she invites us to throw off her yoke, and to make her our servant. Is this the invitation which the master gives his slaves? Is it his aim to awaken the powers of those on whom he lays his burdens, and to give them increasing mastery over himself? Is it not his aim to curb their will, break their spirits, and shut them up for ever in the same narrow and degrading work? Oh, let not nature be profaned, let not her parental rule be blasphemed, by comparing with her the slaveholder!

2. Having considered the moral influence of slavery, I proceed to consider its Intellectual influence, another great topic. God gave us intellectual power, that it should be cultivated; and a system which degrades it, and can only be upheld by its depression, opposes one of his most benevolent designs. Reason is God's image in man, and the capacity of acquiring truth is among his best inspirations. To call forth the intellect is a principal purpose of the circumstances in which we are placed, of the child's connexion with the parent, and of the necessity laid on him in maturer life to provide for himself and others. The education of the intellect is not confined to youth; but the various experience of later years does vastly more than books and colleges to ripen and invigorate the faculties.

Now, the whole lot of the slave is fitted to keep his mind in childhood and bondage. Though living in a land of light, few beams find their way to his benighted understanding. No parent feels the duty of instructing him. No teacher is provided for him, but the Driver, who breaks him, almost in childhood, to the servile tasks which are to fill up his life. No book is opened to his youthful curiosity. As he advances in years, no new excitements supply the place of teachers. He is not cast on himself, made to depend on his own energies. No stirring prizes in life awaken his dormant faculties. Fed and clothed by others like a child, directed in every step, doomed for life to a monotonous round of labor, he lives and dies without a spring to his powers, often brutally unconscious of his spiritual nature. Nor is this all. When benevolence would approach him with instruction, it is repelled. He is not allowed to be taught. The light is jealously barred out. The voice, which would speak to him as a man, is put to silence. He must not even be enabled to read the word of God. His immortal spirit is systematically crushed.

It is said, I know, that the ignorance of the slave is necessary to the security of the master, and the quiet of the state; and this is said truly. Slavery and knowledge cannot live together. To enlighten the slave is to break his chain. To make him harmless, he must be kept blind. He cannot be left to read in an enlightened age, without endangering his master; for what can he read which will not give, at least, some hint of his wrongs? Should his eye chance to fall on " the Declaration of Independance," how would the truth glare on him, " that all men are born free and equal"! All knowledge furnishes arguments against slavery. From every subject light would break forth to reveal his inalienable and outraged rights. The very exercise of his intellect would give him the conciousness of being made for something more than a slave. I agree to the necessity laid on his master to keep him in darkness. And what stronger argument against slavery can be conceived? It compels the master to degrade, systematically, the mind of the slave; to war against human intelligence; to resist that improvement which is the end of the Creator. "Wo to him that taketh away the key of knowledge!" To kill the body is a great crime. The Spirit we cannot kill, but we can bury it in deathlike lethargy ; and is this a light crime in the sight of its Maker ?

Let it not be said, that almost every where the laboring classes are doomed to ignorance, deprived of the means of instruction. The intellectual advantages of the laboring freeman, who is entrusted with the care of himself, raise him far above the slave; and, accordingly, superior minds are constantly seen to issue from the less educated classes. Besides, in free communities, philanthropy is not forbidden to labor for the improvement of the ignorant. The obligation of the prosperous and instructed to elevate their less favored brethren is taught, and not taught in vain. Benevolence is making perpetual encroachments on the domain of ignorance and crime. In communities, on the other hand, cursed with slavery, half the population, sometimes more, are given up, intentionally and systematically, to hopeless ignorance. To raise this mass to intelligence and self government is a crime. The sentence of perpetual degradation is passed on a large portion of the human race. In this view, how great the ill desert of slavery!

3. I proceed, now, to the Domestic influences of slavery; and here we must look for a dark picture. Slavery virtually dissolves the domestic relations. It ruptures the most sacred ties on earth. It violates home. It lacerates the best affections. The domestic relations precede, and, in our present existence, are worth more than all our other social ties. They give the first throb to the heart, and unseal the deep fountains of its love. Home is the chief school of human virtue. Its responsibilities, joys, sorrows, smiles, tears, hopes, and solicitudes, form the chief interests of human life. Go where a man may, home is the centre to which his heart turns. The thought of his home nerves his arm and lightens his toil. For that his heart yearns, when he is far off. There he garners up his best treasures. God has ordained for all men alike the highest earthly happiness, in providing for all the sanctuary of home. But the slave's home does not merit the name. To him it is no sanctuary. It is open to violation, insult, outrage. His children belong to another, are provided for by another, are disposed of by another. The most precious burden with which the heart can be charged, the happiness of

his child, he must not bear. He lives not for his family, but for a stranger. He cannot improve their lot. His wife and daughter he cannot shield from insult. They may be torn from him at another's pleasure, sold as beasts of burden, sent he knows not whither, sent where he cannot reach them, or even interchange inquiries and messages of love. To the slave marriage has no sanctity. It may be dissolved in a moment at another's will. His wife, son, and daughter may be lashed before his eyes, and not a finger must be lifted in their defence. He sees the scar of the lash on his wife and child. Thus the slave's home is desecrated. Thus the tenderest relations, intended by God equally for all, and intended to be the chief springs of happiness and virtue, are sported with wantonly and cruelly. What outrage so great as to enter a man's house, and tear from his side the beings whom God has bound to him by the holiest ties? Every man can make the case his own. Every mother can bring it home to her own heart.

And let it not be said that the slave has not the sensibilities of other men. Nature is too strong even for slavery to conquor. Even the brute has the yearnings of parental love. But suppose that the conjugal and parental ties of the slave may be severed without a pang. What a curse must be slavery, if it can so blight the heart with more than brutal insensibility, if it can sink the human mother below the polar she-bear, which "howls and dies for her sundered cub!" But it does not and cannot turn the slave to stone. It leaves, at least, feeling enough to make these domestic wrongs occasions of frequent and deep suffering. Still it must do much to quench the natural affections. Can the wife, who has been brought under influences most unfriendly to female purity and honor, who is exposed to the whip, who may be torn away at her master's will, and whose support and protection are not committed to a husband's faithfulness, can such a wife, if the name may be given her, be loved and honored as a woman should be? Or can the love which should bind together man and his offspring, be expected, under an institution, which subverts, in a great degree, filial dependence and parental authority and care? Slavery withers the affections and happiness of home at their very root, by tainting female purity.

Woman, brought up in degradation, placed under another's power and at another's disposal, and never taught to look forward to the happiness of an inviolate, honorable marriage, can hardly possess the feelings and virtues of her sex. A blight falls on her in her early years. Those who have daughters can comprehend her lot. In truth, licentiousness among bond and free is the natural issue of all-polluting slavery. Domestic happiness perishes under its touch, both among bond and free.

How wonderful is it, that in civilized countries men can be so steeled by habit as to invade without remorse the peace, purity, and sacred relations of domestic life, as to put asunder those whom God has joined together, as to break up households by processes more painful than death! And this is done for pecuniary profit! What! Can men, having human feeling, grow rich by the desolation of families? We hear of some of the Southern States enriching themselves by breeding slaves for sale. Of all the licensed occupations of society this is the most detestable. What! Grow men, like cattle! Rear human families, like herds of swine, and then scatter them to the four winds for gain! Among the imprecations uttered by man on man, is there one more fearful, more ominous, than the sighing of the mother bereft of her child by unfeeling cupidity? If blood cry to God, surely that sigh will be heard in heaven.

Let it not be said that members of families are often separated in all conditions of life. Yes, but separated under the influence of love. The husband leaves wife and children, that he may provide for their support, and carries them with him in his heart and hopes. The sailor, in his lonely night-watch, looks homeward, and well known voices come to him amidst the roar of the waves. The parent sends away his children, but sends them to prosper, and to press them again to his heart with a joy enhanced by separation. Are such the separations which slavery makes? And can he, who has scattered other families, ask God to bless his own?

4. I proceed to another important view of the evils of slavery. Slavery produces and gives license to Cruelty. By this it is not meant that cruelty is the universal, habitual, unfail-

ing result. Thanks to God, Christianity has not entered the world in vain. Where it has not cast down, it has mitigated bad institutions. Slavery in this country differs widely from that of ancient times, and from that which the Spaniards imposed on the aboriginals of South America. There is here an increasing disposition to multiply the comforts of the slaves, and in this let us rejoice. At the same time, we must remember, that, under the light of the present day, and in a country where Christianity and the rights of men are understood, a diminished severity may contain more guilt than the ferocity of darker ages. Cruelty in its lighter forms is now a greater crime than the atrocious usages of antiquity at which we shudder. "The times of that ignorance God winked at, but *now* he calleth men every where to repent." It should also be considered that the slightest cruelty to the slave is an aggravated wrong, because he is unjustly held in bondage, unjustly held as property. We condemn the man who enforces harshly a righteous claim. What, then, ought we to think of lashing and scarring fellow-creatures, for the purpose of upholding an unrighteous, usurped power, of extorting labor which is not our due?

I have said that cruelty is not the habit of the slave States of this country. Still, that it is frequent we cannot doubt. Reports, which harrow up our souls, come to us from that quarter; and we know that they must be essentially correct, because it is impossible that a large part, perhaps the majority, of the population of a country can be broken to passive, unlimited submission, without examples of terrible severity.

Let it not be said, as is sometimes done, that cruel deeds are perpetrated every where else, as well as in slave-countries. Be it so; but in all civilized nations unscourged by slavery, a principal object of legislation is to protect every man from cruelty, and to bring every man to punishment, who wantonly tortures or wounds another; whilst slavery plucks off restraint from the ferocious, or leaves them to satiate their rage with impunity.—Let it not be said that these barbarities are regarded no where with more horror than at the South. Be it so. They are abhorred, but allowed. The power of individuals to lacerate their fellow-creatures is given to them by the community. The community abhors the abuse, but confers the power which will certainly be abused, and thus strips itself of all defence before the bar of Almighty Justice. It must answer for the crimes which are shielded by its laws. —Let it not be said, that these cruelties are checked by the private interest of the slave-holder. Does regard to private interest save from brutal treatment the draught-horse in our streets? And may not a vast amount of suffering be inflicted, which will not put in peril the life or strength of the slave?

To substantiate the charge of cruelty, I shall not, as I have said, have recourse to current reports, however well established. I am willing to dismiss them all as false. I stand on other ground. Reports may lie, but our daily experience of human nature cannot lie. I summon no witnesses, or rather I appeal to a witness every where present, a witness in every heart. Who that has watched his own heart, or observed others, does not feel that man is not fit to be trusted with absolute, irresponsible power over men? It must be abused. The selfish passions and pride of our nature will as surely abuse it, as the storm will ravage, or the ocean swell and roar under the whirlwind. A being, so ignorant, so headstrong, so passionate, as man, ought not to be trusted with this terrible dominion. He ought not to desire it. He ought to dread it. He ought to cast it from him, as most perilous to himself and others.

Absolute power was not meant for man. There is, indeed, an exception to this rule. There is one case, in which God puts a human being wholly defenceless into another's hands. I refer to the child, who is wholly subjected to the parent's will. But observe how carefully, I might almost say anxiously, God has provided against the abuse of this power. He has raised up in the heart of the parent a friend, a guardian, whom the mightiest on earth cannot resist. He has fitted the parent for this trust, by teaching him to love his child better than himself. No eloquence on earth is so subduing as the moaning of the infant when in pain. No reward is sweeter than that infant's smile. We say, God has put the infant into the parent's hands. Might we not more truly say, that he has put the parent into the child's power? That little being sends forth his father to toil, and makes the mother

D

watch over him by day, and fix on him her sleepless eyes by night. No tyrant lays such a yoke. Thus God has fenced and secured from abuse the power of the parent; and yet even the parent has been known, in a moment of passion, to be cruel to his child. Is man, then, to be trusted with absolute power over a fellow-creature, who, instead of being commended by nature to his tenderest love, belongs to a despised race, is regarded as property, is made the passive instrument of his gratification and gain? I ask no documents to prove the abuses of this power, nor do I care what is said to disprove them. Millions may rise up and tell me that the slave suffers little from cruelty. I know too much of human nature, human history, human passion to believe them. I acquit slave-holders of all peculiar depravity. I judge them by myself. I say, that absolute power always corrupts human nature more or less. I say, that extraordinary, almost miraculous self-control is necessary to secure the slave-holder from provocation and passion; and is self-control the virtue which above all others grows up amidst the possession of irresponsible dominion? Even when the slave-holder honestly acquits himself of cruelty, he may be criminal. His own consciousness is to be distrusted. Having begun with wronging the slave, with wresting from him sacred rights, he may be expected to multiply wrongs without thought. The degraded state of the slave may induce in the master a mode of treatment essentially inhuman and insulting, but which he never dreams to be cruel. The influence of slavery in indurating the moral feeling and blinding men to wrongs is one of its worst evils.

But suppose the master to be ever so humane. Still, he is not always watching over his slave. He has his pleasures to attend to. He is often absent. His terrible power must be delegated. And to whom is it delegated? To men prepared to govern others, by having learned to govern themselves? To men having a deep interest in the slaves? To wise men, instructed in human nature? To Christians, trained to purity and love? Who does not know, that the office of Overseer is among the last, which an enlightened, philanthropic, self-respecting man would choose? Who does not know, how often the overseer pollutes the plantation by his licentiousness, as well as scourges it by his severity? In the hands of such a man the lash is placed. To such a man is committed the most fearful trust on earth! For his cruelties the master must answer, as truly as if they were his own. Nor is this all. The master does more than delegate his power to the overseer. How often does he part with it wholly to the slave-dealer! And has he weighed the responsibility of such a transfer? Does he not know, that, in selling his slaves into merciless hands, he is merciless himself, and must give an account to God for every barbarity of which they become the victims? The notorious cruelty of the slave-dealers can be no false report, for it belongs to their vocation. These are the men, who throng and defile our Seat of Government, whose slave-markets and slave-dungeons turn to mockery the language of freedom in the halls of Congress, and who make us justly the by-word and the scorn of the nations. Is there no cruelty in putting slaves under the bloody lash of the slave-dealer, to be driven like herds of cattle to distant regions, and there to pass into the hands of strangers, without a pledge of their finding justice or mercy? What heart, not seared by custom, would not recoil from such barbarity?

It has been seen that I do not ground my argument at all on cases of excessive cruelty. I should attach less importance to these than do most persons, even were they more frequent. They form a very, very small account of suffering, compared with what is inflicted by abuses of power too minute for notice. Blows, insults, privations, which make no noise, and leave no scar, are incomparably more destructive of happiness than a few brutal violences which move general indignation. A weak, despised being, having no means of defence or redress, living in a community armed against his rights, regarded as property, and as bound to entire, unresisting compliance with another's will, if not subjected to inflictions of ferocious cruelty, is yet exposed to less striking and shocking forms of cruelty, the amount of which must be a fearful mass of suffering.

But could it be proved that there are no cruelties in slave-countries, we ought not then to be more reconciled to slavery than we now are. For what would this shew? That cruelty is not needed. And why not needed? Because the slave is

entirely subdued to his lot. No man will be wholly unresisting in bondage, but he who is thoroughly imbued with the
spirit of a slave. If the colored race never need punishment,
it is because the feelings of men are dead within them, because they have no consciousness of rights, because they are
cowards, without respect for themselves, and without confidence in the sharers of their degraded lot. The quiet of slavery is like that which the Roman legions left in ancient
Britain, the stillness of death. Why were the Romans accustomed to work their slaves in chains by day, and confine
them in dungeons by night? Not because they loved cruelty
for its own sake; but because their slaves were stung with a
consciousness of degradation, because they brought from the
forests of Dacia some rude ideas of human dignity, or from
civilized countries some experience of social improvements,
which naturally issued in violence and exasperation. They
needed cruelty, for their own wills were not broken to another's, and the spirit of freemen was not wholly gone. The
slave *must* meet cruel treatment either inwardly or outwardly.
Either the soul or the body must receive the blow. Either
the flesh must be tortured or the spirit struck down. Dread-
ful alternative to which slavery is reduced !

5. I proceed to one more view of the evils of slavery. I
refer to its influence on the Master. This topic cannot, perhaps, be so handled as to avoid giving offence; but without
it an imperfect view of the subject would be given. I will
pass over many views. I will say nothing of the tendency of
slavery to unsettle the ideas of Right in the slave-holder, to
impair his convictions of Justice and Benevolence; or of its
tendency to associate with labor ideas of degradation, and to
recommend idleness as an honorable exemption. I will confine myself to two considerations.

The first is, that slavery, above all other influences, nou-
rishes the passion for power and its kindred vices. There is
no passion which needs a stronger curb. Men's worst crimes
have sprung from the desire of being masters, of bending
others to their yoke. And the natural tendency of bringing
others into subjection to our absolute will is to quicken into
fearful activity the imperious, haughty, proud, self-seeking

propensities of our nature. Man cannot, without imminent peril to his virtue, own a fellow-creature, or use the word of absolute command to his brethren. God never delegated this power. It is an usurpation of the Divine dominion, and its natural influence is to produce a spirit of superiority to divine as well as to human laws.

Undoubtedly this tendency is in a measure counteracted by the spirit of the age and the genius of Christianity, and in conscientious individuals it may be wholly overcome; but we see its fruits in the corruptions of moral sentiment which prevail among slave-holders. A quick resentment of whatever is thought to encroach on personal dignity, a trembling jealousy of reputation, vehemence of the vindictive passions, and contempt of all laws, human and divine, in retaliating injury,—these take rank among the virtues of men whose self-estimation has been fed by the possession of absolute power.

Of consequence the direct tendency of slavery is to annihilate the control of Christianity. Humility is by eminence the spirit of Christianity. No vice was so severely rebuked by our Lord, as the passion for ruling over others. A deference towards all human beings as our brethren, a benevolence which disposes us to serve rather than to reign, to concede our own rather than to encroach on others' rights, to forgive, not avenge wrongs, to govern our own spirits instead of breaking the spirit of an inferior or foe,—this is Christianity; a religion too high and pure to be understood and obeyed any where as it should be, but which meets singular hostility in the habits and mind generated by slavery.

The slave-holder, indeed, values himself on his loftiness of spirit. He has a consciousness of dignity, which imposes on himself and others. But truth cannot stoop to this lofty mien. Truth, moral, Christian truth, condemns it, and condemns those who bow to it. Self-respect, founded on a consciousness of our moral nature and immortal destiny, is, indeed, a noble principle; but this sentiment includes, as a part of itself, respect for all who partake our nature. A consciousness of dignity, founded on the subjection of others to our absolute will, is inhuman and unjust. It is time that the teachings of Christ were understood. In proportion as a man acquires a lofty bearing from the habit of command over wronged and depressed fellow-creatures, so far he casts away true honor, so far he has fallen in the sight of God and Virtue.

I approach a more delicate subject, and one on which I shall not enlarge. To own the persons of others, to hold females in slavery, is necessarily fatal to the purity of a people. That unprotected females, stripped by their degraded condition of woman's self-respect, should be used to minister to other passions in men than the love of gain, is next to inevitable. Accordingly, in such a community the reins are given to youthful licentiousness. Youth, every where in perils, is in these circumstances urged to vice with a terrible power. And the evil cannot stop at youth. Early licentiousness is fruitful of crime in mature life. How far the obligation to conjugal fidelity, the sacredness of domestic ties, will be revered amidst such habits, such temptations, such facilities to vice, as are involved in slavery, needs no exposition. So terrible is the connexion of crimes! They who invade the domestic rights of others, suffer in their own homes. The household of the slave may be broken up arbitrarily by the master; but he finds his revenge, if revenge he asks, in the blight which the master's unfaithfulness sheds over his own domestic joys. A slave-country reeks with licentiousness. It is tainted with a deadlier pestilence than the plague.

But the worst is not told. As a consequence of criminal connexions, many a master has children born into slavery. Of these, most, I presume, receive protection, perhaps indulgence, during the life of the fathers ; but at their death, not a few are left to the chances of a cruel bondage. These cases must have increased, since the difficulties of emancipation have even multiplied. Still more, it is to be feared, that there are cases, in which the master puts his own children under the whip of the overseer, or else sells them to undergo the miseries of bondage among strangers. I should rejoice to learn that my impressions on this point are false. If they be true, then our own country, calling itself enlightened and Christian, is defiled with one of the greatest enormities on earth. We send missionaries to heathen lands. Among the pollutions of heathenism I know nothing worse than this.

The heathen, who feasts on his country's foe, may hold up his head by the side of the Christian who sells his child for gain, sells him to be a slave. God forbid that I should charge this crime on a people! But however rarely it may occur, it is a fruit of slavery, an exercise of power belonging to slavery, and no laws restrain or punish it. Such are the evils which spring naturally from the licentiousness generated by slavery.

I have now placed before the reader the chief evils of slavery. We are told, however, that these are not without mitigation, that slavery has advantages which do much to counterbalance its wrongs and pains. Not a few are partially reconciled to the institution by the language of confidence in which its benefits are sometimes announced. I shall therefore close this chapter with a very brief consideration of what are thought to be the advantages of slavery.

It it often said, that the slave does less work than the free laborer. He bears a lighter burden than liberty would lay on him. Perhaps this is generally true; yet when circumstances promise profit to the master from the imposition of excessive labor, the slave is not spared. In the West Indies, the terrible waste of life among the overworked cultivators required large supplies from Africa to keep up the failing population. In this country it is probably true that the slave works less than the free laborer; but it does not therefore follow that his work is lighter. For what is it that lightens toil? It is Hope; it is Love; it is Strong Motive. That labor is light, which we do from the heart; to which a great good quickens us; which is to better our lot. That labor is light, which is to comfort, adorn, and cheer our homes, to give instruction to our children, to solace the declining years of a parent, to give to our grateful and generous sentiments the means of exertion. Great effort from great motives is the best definition of a happy life. The easiest labor is a burden to him who has no motive for performing it. How wearisome is the task imposed by another, and wrongfully imposed! The slave cannot easily be made to do a freeman's work; and why? because he wants a freeman's spirit, because the spring of labor is impaired within him, because he works as a machine, not a free agent. The compulsion, under which he toils for another, takes from labor its sweetness, makes the daily round of life arid and dull, makes escape from toil the chief interest of life.

We are farther told that the slave is freed from all care, that he is sure of future support, that when old he is not dismissed to the poor house, but fed and sheltered in his own hut. This is true; but it is also true that nothing can be gained by violating the great laws and essential rights of our nature. The slave, we are told, has no care, his future is provided for. Yet God created him to provide for the future, to take care of his own happiness; and he cannot be freed from this care without injury to his moral and intellectual life. Why has God given foresight and power over the future, but to be used? Is it a blessing to a rational creature, to be placed in a condition which chains his faculties to the present moment, which leaves nothing before him to rouse the intellect or touch the heart? Be it also remembered, that the same provision, which relieves the slave from anxiety, cuts him off from hope. The future is not, indeed, haunted by spectres of poverty, nor is it brightened by images of joy. It stretches before him sterile, monotonous, expanding into no refreshing verdure, and sending no cheering whisper of a better lot.

It is true that the free laborer may become a pauper; and so may the free rich man, both of the North and the South. Still, our capitalists never dream of flying to slavery as a security against the almshouse. Freedom undoubtedly has its perils. It offers nothing to the slothful and dissolute. Among a people left to seek their own good in their own way, some of all classes fail from vice, some from incapacity, some from misfortune. All classes will furnish members to the body of the poor. But in this country the number is small, and ought constantly to decrease. The evil, however lamentable, is not so remediless and spreading as to furnish a motive for reducing half the population to chains. Benevolence does much to mitigate it. The best minds are inquiring how it may be prevented, diminished, removed. It is giving excitement to a philanthropy which creates out of misfortune new bonds of union between man and man.

Our slave-holding brethren, who tell us that the condition

of the slave is better than that of the free laborer at the North, talk ignorantly and rashly. They do not, cannot know, what to us is matter of daily observation, that from the families of our farmers and mechanics have sprung our most distinguished men, men who have done most for science, arts, letters, religion, and freedom; and that the noblest spirits among us would have been lost to their country and mankind, had the laboring class here been doomed to slavery. They do not know, what we rejoice to tell them, that this class partakes largely of the impulse given to the whole community; that the means of intellectual improvement are multiplying to the laborious as fast as to the opulent; that our most distinguished citizens meet them as brethren, and communicate to them in public discourses their own most important acquisitions. Undoubtedly, the Christian, republican spirit is not working, even here, as it should. The more improved and prosperous classes have not yet learned that it is their great mission to elevate morally and intellectually the less advanced classes of the community; but the great truth is more and more recognised, and accordingly a new era may be said to be opening on society.

It is said, however, that the slave, if not to be compared to the free laborer at the North, is in a happier condition, than the Irish peasantry. Let this be granted. Let the security of the peasant's domestic relations, let his church, and his school-house, and his faint hope of a better lot pass for nothing. Because Ireland is suffering from the mis-government and oppression of ages, does it follow that a less grinding oppression is a good? Besides, are not the wrongs of Ireland acknowledged? Is not British legislation laboring to restore her prosperity? Is it not true, that, whilst the slave's lot admits no important change, the most enlightened minds are at work to confer on the Irish peasant the blessings of education, of equal laws, of new springs to exertion, of new sources of wealth? Other men, however fallen, may be lifted up. An immovable weight presses on the slave.

But still we are told the slave is gay. He is not as wretched as our theories teach. After his toil, he sings, he dances, he gives no signs of an exhausted frame or gloomy spirit. The slave happy! Why, then, contend for Rights? Why follow with beating hearts the struggles of the patriot for freedom? Why canonize the martyr to freedom? The slave happy! Then happiness is to be found in giving up the distinctive attributes of a man; in darkening intellect and conscience; in quenching generous sentiments; in servility of spirit; in living under a whip; in having neither property nor rights; in holding wife and child at another's pleasure; in toiling without hope; in living without an end! The slave, indeed, has his pleasures. His animal nature survives the injury to his rational and moral powers; and every animal has its enjoyments. The kindness of Providence allows no human being to be wholly divorced from good. The lamb frolics; the dog leaps for joy; the bird fills the air with cheerful harmony; and the slave spends his holiday in laughter and the dance. Thanks to Him who never leaves himself without witness; who cheers even the desert with spots of verdure; and opens a fountain of joy in the most withered heart! It is not possible, however, to contemplate the occasional gaiety of the slave without some mixture of painful thought. He is gay, because he has not learned to think; because he is too fallen to feel his wrongs; because he wants just self-respect. We are grieved by the gaiety of the insane. There is a sadness in the gaiety of him, whose lightness of heart would be turned to bitterness and indignation, were one ray of light to awaken in him the spirit of a man.

That there are those among the free, who are more wretched than slaves, is undoubtedly true; just as there is incomparably greater misery among men than among brutes. The brute never knew the agony of a human spirit torn by remorse or wounded in its love. But would we cease to be human, because our capacity for suffering increases with the elevation of our nature? All blessings may be perverted, and the greatest perverted most. Were we to visit a slave-country, undoubtedly the most miserable human beings would be found among the free; for among them the passions have wider sweep, and the power they possess may be used to their own ruin. Liberty is not a necessity of happiness. It is only a means of good. It is a trust which may be abused. Are all such trusts to be cast away? Are they not the greatest gifts of Heaven?

But the slave, we are told, often manifests affection to his master, grieves at his departure, and welcomes his return. I will not endeavour to explain this, by saying that the master's absence places the slave under the overseer. Nor will I object, that the slave's propensity to steal from his master, his need of the whip to urge him to toil, and the dread of insurrection which he inspires, are signs of any thing but love. There is, undoubtedly, much more affection in this relation than could be expected. Of all races of men, the African is the mildest and most susceptible of attachment. He loves, where the European would hate. He watches the life of a master, whom the North-American Indian, in like circumstances, would stab to the heart. The African is affectionate. Is this a reason for holding him in chains? We cannot however, think of this most interesting feature of slavery with unmixed pleasure. It is the curse of slavery, that it can touch nothing which it does not debase. Even love, that sentiment given us by God to be the germ of a divine virtue, becomes in the slave a weakness, almost a degradation. His affections lose much of their beauty and dignity. He ought, indeed, to feel benevolence towards his master; but to attach himself to man who keeps him in the dust and denies him the rights of a man; to be grateful and devoted to one who extorts his toil and debases him into a chattel; this has a taint of servility, which makes us grieve whilst we admire. However, we would not diminish the attachment of the slave. He is the happier for his generosity. Let him love his master, and let the master win love by kindness. We only say, let not this manifestation of a generous nature in the slave be turned against him. Let it not be made an answer to an exposition of his wrongs. Let it not be used as a weapon for his perpetual degradation.

But the slave, we are told, is taught Religion. This is the most cheering sound which comes to us from the land of bondage. We are rejoiced to learn that any portion of the slaves are instructed in that truth, which gives inward freedom. They hear at least one voice of deep, genuine love, the voice of Christ; and read in his cross what all other things hide from them, the unutterable worth of their spiritual nature. This portion, however, is small. The greater part are still buried in heathen ignorance. Besides, Religion, though a great good, can hardly exert its full power on the slave. Will it not be taught to make him obedient to his master, rather than to raise him to the dignity of a man? Is slavery, which tends so proverbially to debase the mind, the preparation for spiritual truth? Can the slave comprehend the principle of Love, the essential principle of Christianity, when he hears it from the lips of those whose relations to him express injustice and selfishness? But suppose him to receive Christianity in its purity, and to feel all its power. Is this to reconcile us to slavery? Is a being, who can understand the sublimest truth which has ever entered the human mind, who can love and adore God, who can conform himself to the celestial virtue of the Saviour, for whom that Saviour died, to whom heaven is opened, whose repentance now gives joy in heaven,—is such a being to be held as property, driven by force as the brute, and denied the rights of man by a fellow-creature, by a professed disciple of the just and merciful Saviour? Has he a religious nature, and dares any one hold him as a slave?

I have now completed my views of the evils of slavery, and have shown how little they are mitigated by what are thought its advantages. In this whole discussion I have cautiously avoided quoting particular examples of its baneful influences. I have not brought together accounts of horrible cruelty which come to us from the South. I have confined myself to the natural tendencies of slavery, to evils bound up in its very nature, which, as long as man is man, cannot be separated from it. That these evils are unmixed or universal, I do not say. There are and must be exceptions to them, and more or less of good may often be found in connexion with them. No institution, be it what it may, can make the life of a human being wholly evil, or cut off every means of improvement. God's benevolence triumphs over all the perverseness and folly of man's devices. He sends a cheering beam into the darkest abode. The slave has his hours of exhilaration. His hut occasionally rings with thoughtless mirth. Among this class, too, there are and must be, occasionally, higher pleasures. God is no respecter of persons; and in some slaves there is a happy nature which no condition can destroy, just as among children we find some whom the worst education cannot spoil. The African is so affectionate, imitative, and docile, that in favorable circumstances he catches much that is good; and accordingly the influence of a wise and kind master will be seen in the very countenance and bearing of his slaves. Among this degraded people, there are, occasionally, examples of superior intelligence and virtue, showing the groundlessness of the opinion that they are incapable of filling a higher rank than slavery, and showing that human nature is too generous and hardy to be wholly destroyed in the most unpropitious state. We also witness in this class, and very often, a superior physical development, a grace of form and motion, which almost extorts a feeling approaching respect. I mean not to affirm that slavery excludes all good, for human life cannot long endure under the privation of every thing happy and improving. I have spoken of its natural tendencies and results. These are wholly and only evil.

I am aware that it will be replied to the views now given of slavery, that persons living at a distance from it cannot comprehend it, that its true character can be learned only from those, who know it practically, and are familiar with its operations. To this I will not reply, that I have seen it near at hand. It is sufficient to reply, that men may lose the power of seeing an object fairly, by being too near as well as by being too remote. The slave-holder is too familiar with slavery to understand it. To be educated in injustice, is almost necessarily to be blinded by it more or less. To exercise usurped power from birth, is the surest way to look upon it as a right and a good. The slave-holder tells us that he only can instruct us about slavery. But suppose that we wished to learn the true character of despotism; should we go to the palace and take the despot as our teacher? Should we pay much heed to his assurance, that he alone could understand the character of absolute power, and that we in a republic could know nothing of the condition of men subjected to irresponsible will? The sad influence of slavery, in darkening the mind which is perpetually conversant with it, is disclosed to us in the recent attempts made at the South to represent this institution as a good. Freemen, who would sooner die than resign their rights, talk of the happiness of those from whom every right is wrested. They talk of the slave as " property," with the same confidence as if this were the holiest claim. This is one of the mournful effects of slavery. It darkens the moral sense of the master. And can men, whose position is so unfavorable to just, impartial judgment, expect us to acquiesce in their views?

There is another reply. If the slave-holding States expect us to admit their views of this institution, they must allow it to be freely discussed among themselves. Of what avail is their testimony in favor of slavery, when not a tongue is allowed to say a word in its condemnation? Of what use is the press, when it can publish only on one side? In the slave-holding States freedom of speech is at an end. Whoever should express among them the sentiments respecting slavery which are universally adopted through the civilized world, would put his life in jeopardy, would probably be flayed or hung. On this great subject, which affects vitally their peace and prosperity, their moral and political interests, no philanthropist, who has come to the truth, can speak his mind. Even the minister of religion, who feels the hostility between slavery and Christianity, dares not speak. His calling might not save him from popular rage. Thus slavery avenges itself. It brings the masters under despotism. It takes away that liberty which a free man prizes as life,—liberty of speech. All this, we are told, is necessary, and so it may be; but an institution imposing such a necessity cannot be a good; and one thing is plain; the testimony of men placed under such restraints cannot be too cautiously received. We have better sources of knowledge. We have the testimony of ages, and the testimony of the unchangeable principles of human nature. These assure us that slavery is " evil, and evil continually."

I ought not to close this head, without acknowledging, (what I cheerfully do,) that in many cases the kindness of masters does much for the mitigation of slavery. Could it be rendered harmless, the efforts of many would not be spared to make it so. It is evil, not through any singular corruption in the slave-holder, but from its own nature, and in spite of all efforts to make it good. It is evil, not because it exists on this or that spot. Were it planted at the North, it would become a greater curse, more hardening and depraving, than it now proves under a milder sky. It is not of the particular form of slavery in this country that I complain. I am willing to allow that it is here comparatively mild; that on many plantations no abuses exist but such as are inseparable from its very nature. The mischief lies in its very nature. " Men do not gather grapes of thorns, or figs of thistles." An institution so founded in wrong, so imbued with injustice, cannot be made a good. It cannot like other institutions be perpetuated by being improved. To improve it, is to prepare the way for its subversion. Every melioration of the slave's lot is a step toward freedom. Slavery is thus radically, essentially evil. Every good man should earnestly pray, and use every virtuous influence, that an institution so blighting to human nature may be brought to an end.

CHAPTER V.

SCRIPTURE.

ATTEMPTS are often made to support slavery by the authority of Revelation. " Slavery," it is said, "is allowed in the
Old Testament, and not condemned in the New. Paul commands slaves to obey. He commands masters, not to release
their slaves, but to treat them justly. Therefore slavery is
right, is sanctified by God's Word." In this age of the world,
and amidst the light which has been thrown on the true interpretation of the Scriptures, such reasoning hardly deserves
notice. A few words only will be offered in reply.

This reasoning proves too much. If usages sanctioned in
the Old Testament and not forbidden in the New are right,
then our moral code will undergo a sad deterioration. Poly-
gamy was allowed to the Israelites, was the practice of the
holiest men, and was common and licensed in the age of the
Apostles. But the Apostles no where condemn it, nor was
the renunciation of it made an essential condition of admission into the Christian church. It is true that in one passage
Christ has condemned it by implication. But is not slavery
condemned by stronger implication in the many passages,
which make the new religion to consist in serving one another, and in doing to others what we would that they should
do to ourselves ? Why may not Scripture be used to stock
our houses with wives as well as with slaves ?

Again. Paul is said to sanction slavery. Let us now ask,
What was slavery in the age of Paul ? It was the slavery,
not so much of black as of white men, not merely of barba-
rians but of Greeks, not merely of the ignorant and debased,
but of the virtuous, educated, and refined. Piracy and conquest were the chief means of supplying the slave-market,
and they heeded neither character nor condition. Sometimes
the greater part of the population of a captured city was sold

into bondage, sometimes the whole, as in the case of Jerusalem. Noble and royal families, the rich and great, the learned and powerful, the philosopher and poet, the wisest and best men, were condemned to the chain. Such was ancient slavery. And this we are told is allowed and confirmed by the Word of God! Had Napoleon, on capturing Berlin or Vienna, doomed most or the whole of their inhabitants to bondage; had he seized on venerable matrons, the mothers of illustrious men, who were reposing after virtuous lives in the bosom of grateful families; had he seized on the delicate, refined, beautiful young woman, whose education had prepared her to grace the sphere in which God had placed her, whose plighted love had opened before her visions of bliss, and over all whose prospects the freshest hopes and most glowing imaginations of early life were breathed; had he seized on the minister of religion, the man of science, the man of genius, the sage, the guides of the world; had he scattered these through the slave-markets of the world, and transferred them to the highest bidders at public auction, the men to be converted into instruments of slavish toil, the women into instruments of lust, and both to endure whatever indignities and tortures absolute power can inflict; we should then have had a picture in the present age of slavery as it existed in the time of Paul. Such slavery we are told was sanctioned by the Apostle! Such we are told he pronounced to be morally right! Had Napoleon sent some cargoes of these victims to these shores, we might have bought them, and degraded the noblest beings to our lowest uses, and might have cited Paul to testify to our innocence! Were an infidel to bring this charge against the Apostle, we should say that he was laboring in his vocation; but that a professed Christian should so insult this sainted philanthropist, this martyr to truth and benevolence, is a sad proof of the power of slavery to blind its supporters to the plainest truth.

Slavery, in the age of the Apostle, had so penetrated society, was so intimately interwoven with it, and the materials of servile war were so abundant, that a religion, preaching freedom to its victims, would have shaken the social fabric to its foundation, and would have armed against itself the whole power of the State. Of consequence Paul did not assail it.

E

He satisfied himself with spreading principles, which however slowly, could not but work its destruction. He commanded Philemon to receive his fugitive slave, Onesimus, "not as a slave, but above a slave, as a brother beloved;" and he commanded masters to give to their slaves that which was "*just and equal;*" thus asserting for the slave the rights of a Christian and a Man; and how, in his circumstances, he could have done more for the subversion of slavery, I do not see.

Let me offer another remark. The perversion of Scripture to the support of slavery is singularly inexcusable in this country. Paul not only commanded slaves to obey their masters. He delivered these precepts: "Let every soul be subject to the higher powers. For there is no power but of God; the powers that be are ordained of God. Whosoever, therefore, resisteth the power, resisteth the ordinance of God; and they that resist shall receive to themselves damnation." This passage was written in the time of Nero. It teaches passive obedience to despotism more strongly than any text teaches the lawfulness of slavery. Accordingly it has been quoted for ages by the supporters of arbitrary power, and made the strong hold of tyranny. Did our fathers acquiesce in the most obvious interpretation of this text? Because the first Christians were taught to obey despotic rule, did our fathers feel as if Christianity had stript men of their rights? Did they argue that tyranny was to be excused, because forcible opposition to it is in most cases wrong? Did they argue that absolute power ceases to be unjust, because, as a general rule, it is the duty of subjects to obey? Did they infer that bad institutions ought to be perpetual, because the subversion of them by force will almost always inflict greater evil than it removes? No; they were wiser interpreters of God's word. They believed that despotism was a wrong, notwithstanding the general obligation upon its subjects to obey; and that whenever a whole people should so feel the wrong as to demand its removal, the time for removing it had fully come. Such is the school in which we here have been brought up. To us, it is no mean proof of the divine original of Christianity, that it teaches human brotherhood and favors human rights; and yet, on the ground of two or three passages, which admit different constructions, we make Christianity the minister of slavery, the forger of chains for those whom it came to make free.

It is a plain rule of scriptural criticism, that particular texts should be interpreted according to the general tenor and spirit of Christianity. And what is the general, the perpetual teaching of Christianity in regard to social duty? "All things whatsoever ye would that men should do to you, do ye even so to them; for this is the law and the prophets." Now does not every man feel that nothing, nothing, could induce him to consent to be a slave? Does he not feel, that, if reduced to this abject lot, his whole nature, his reason, conscience, affections, would cry out against it as the greatest of calamities and wrongs? Can he pretend, then, that in holding others in bondage he does to his neighbour what he would that his neighbour should do to him? Of what avail are a few texts, which were designed for local and temporary use, when urged against the vital, essential spirit, and the plainest precepts of our religion?

I close this section with a few extracts from a recent work of one of our most distinguished writers; not that I think additional arguments necessary, but because the authority of Scripture is more sucessfully used than any thing else to reconcile good minds to slavery.

"The very course, which the Gospel takes on this subject, seems to have been the only one that could have been taken in order to effect the universal abolition of slavery. The gospel was designed, not for one race, or for one time, but for all men and for all times. It looked not at the abolition of this form of evil for that age alone, but for its universal abolition. Hence the important object of its author was to gain it a lodgment in every part of the known world; so that, by its universal diffusion among all classes of society, it might quietly and peacefully modify and subdue the evil passions of men; and thus, without violence work a revolution in the whole mass of mankind. In this manner alone could its object, a universal moral revolution, have been accomplished. For if it had forbidden the *evil* instead of subverting the *principle*, if it had proclaimed the unlawfulness of slavery, and taught slaves to *resist* the oppression of their masters, it would instantly have arrayed the two parties in deadly hostility throughout the civilized world; its announcement would have been the signal of servile war; and the very name of the Christian religion would have been forgotten amidst the agitations of universal bloodshed. The fact, under these circumstances, that the Gospel does not forbid slavery, affords no reason to suppose that it does not mean to prohibit it; much less does it afford ground for belief that Jesus Christ intended to authorize it."

"It is important to remember that two grounds of moral obligation are distinctly recognised in the Gospel. The first is our duty to man as man; that is, on the ground of the relation which men sustain to each other; the second is our duty to man as a creature of God; that is, on the relation which we all sustain to God.—Now, it is to be observed, that it is precisely upon this latter ground that the slave is commanded to obey his master. It is never urged like the duty to obedience to parents, because it is right, but because the cultivation of meekness and forbearance under injury will be well pleasing unto God.—The manner in which the duty of servants or slaves is inculcated, therefore, affords no ground for the assertion that the Gospel authorizes one man to hold another in bondage, any more than the command to honor the king, when that king was Nero, authorized the tyranny of the emperor; or than the command to turn the other cheek, when one is smitten, justifies the infliction of violence by an injurious man."*

---

*Wayland's Elements of Moral Science, pages 225—6. The discussion of Slavery, in the chapter from which these extracts are made, is well worthy attention.

CHAPTER VI.

MEANS OF REMOVING SLAVERY.

How slavery shall be removed, is a question for the slave-holder, and one which he alone can fully answer. He alone has an intimate knowledge of the character and habits of the slaves, to which the means of emancipation should be carefully adapted. General views and principles may and should be suggested at a distance; but the mode of applying them can be understood only by those who dwell on the spot where the evil exists. To the slaveholder belongs the duty of settling and employing the best methods of liberation, and to no other. We have no right of interference, nor do we desire it. We hold that the dangers of emancipation, if such there are, would be indefinitely increased, were the boon to come to the slave from a foreign hand, were he to see it forced on the master by a foreign power. It is of the highest importance, that slavery should be succeeded by a friendly relation between master and slave; and to produce this, the latter must see in the former his benefactor and deliverer. His liberty must seem to him an expression of benevolence and regard for his rights. He must put confidence in his superiors, and look to them cheerfully and gratefully for counsel and aid. Let him feel, that liberty has been wrung from an unwilling master, who would willingly replace the chain, and jealousy, vindic·tiveness, and hatred would spring up, to blight the innocence and happiness of his new freedom, and to make it a peril to himself and all around him. I believe, indeed, that emancipation, though so bestowed, would be better than everlasting bondage; but the responsibility of so conferring it is one that none of us are anxious to assume.

We cannot but fear much from the experiment now in progress in the West Indies, on account of its being the work fo a foreign hand. The planters, especially of Jamaica, have opposed the mother-country with a pertinaciousness bordering on insanity; have done much to exasperate the slaves, whose freedom they could not prevent; have done nothing to prepare them for liberty; have met them with gloom on their countenances, and with evil auguries on their lips; have taught them to look abroad for relief, and to see in their masters only obstructions to the amelioration of their lot. It is possible that under all these obstacles emancipation may succeed. God grant it success! If it fail, the planter will have brought the ruin very much on himself. Policy, as well as duty, so plainly taught him to take into his own hands the work which a superior power had begun, to spare no effort, no expense, for binding to him by new ties those who were to throw off their former chains, that we know not how to account for his conduct, but by supposing that his unhappy position as a slaveholder had robbed him of his reason, as well as blunted his moral sense.

In this country no power but that of the slaveholding States can remove the evil, and none of us are anxious to take the office from their hands. They alone can do it safely. They alone can determine and apply the true and sure means of emancipation. That such means exist I cannot doubt; for emancipation has already been carried through successfully in other countries; and even were there no precedent, I should be sure, that, under God's benevolent and righteous government, there could not be a necessity for holding human beings in perpetual bondage. This faith, however, is not universal. Many, when they hear of the evils of slavery, say, "It is bad, but remediless. There are no means of relief." They say, in a despairing tone, "Give us your plan;" and justify their indifference to emancipation, by what they call its hopelessness. This state of mind has induced me to offer a few remarks on the means of removing slavery; not that I suppose, that an individual so distant can do the work to which the whole intellect and benevolence of the South should be summoned, but that I may suggest a few principles, which I think would insure a happy result to the benevolent enterprise, and that I may remove the incredulity of which I have complained.

What, then, is to be done for the removal of slavery? In the first place, the slaveholders should solemnly disclaim the right of property in human beings. The great principle, that man cannot belong to man, should be distinctly, solemnly recognised. The slave should be acknowledged as a partaker of a common nature, as having the essential rights of humanity. This great truth lies at the foundation of every wise plan for his relief. The cordial admission of it would give a consciousness of dignity, of grandeur, to efforts for emancipation. There is, indeed, a grandeur in the idea of raising more than two millions of human beings to the enjoyment of human rights, to the blessings of Christian civilization, to the means of indefinite improvement. The slaveholding States are called to a nobler work of benevolence than is committed to any other communities. They should comprehend its dignity. This they cannot do, till the slave is truly, sincerely, with the mind and heart, recognised as a Man, till he ceases to be regarded as Property.

It may be asked, whether, in calling the slaveholding States to abolish property in the slave, I intend that he should be immediately set free from all his present restraints. By no means. Nothing is farther from my thoughts. The slave cannot rightfully, and should not be owned by the Individual. But, like every other citizen, he belongs to the Community, he is subject to the community, and the community has a right and is bound to continue all such restraints, as its own safety and the well-being of the slave demand. It would be cruelty, not kindness, to the latter, to give him a freedom, which he is unprepared to understand or enjoy. It would be cruelty to strike the fetters from a man, whose first steps would infallibly lead him to a precipice. The slave should not have an owner, but he should have a guardian. He needs authority, to supply the lack of that discretion which he has not yet attained; but it should be the authority of a friend; an official authority, conferred by the state, and for which there should be responsibleness to the state, an authority especially designed to prepare its subjects for personal freedom. The slave should not, in the first instance, be allowed to wander at his will, beyond the plantation on which he toils; and if he cannot be induced to work by rational and natural motives, he should be obliged to labor; on the same principles on which the vagrant in other communities is confined and compelled to earn his bread. The gift of liberty would be a mere name, and worse than nominal, were he to be let loose on society under circumstances driving him to crimes, for which he would be condemned to severer bondage than he had escaped. Many restraints must be continued; but continued, not because the colored race are property, not because they are bound to live and toil for an owner, but solely and wholly because their own innocence, security, and education, and the public order and peace, require them, during the present incapacity, to be restrained. It should be remembered, that this incapacity is not their fault, but their misfortune; not they, but the community, are responsible for it; and that the community cannot, without crime, profit by its own wrong. If the government should make any distinctions among the citizens, it should be in behalf of the injured. Instead of urging the past existence of slavery, and the incapacity which it has induced, as apologies or reasons for continuing the yoke, the community should find in these very circumstances new obligations to effort for the wronged.

There is but one weighty argument against immediate emancipation, namely, that the slave would not support himself and his children by honest industry; that, having always worked on compulsion, he will not work without it; that, having always labored from another's will, he will not labor from his own; that there is no spring of exertion in his own mind; that he is unused to forethought, providence, and self-denial, and the responsibilities of domestic life; that freedom would produce idleness; idleness, want; want, crime; and that crime, when it should become the habit of numbers, would bring misery, perhaps ruin, not only on the offenders, but the state. Here lies the strength of the argument for continuing present restraint. Give the slaves disposition and power to support themselves and their families by honest industry, and complete emancipation should not be delayed one hour.

The great step, then, towards the removal of slavery is to prepare the slaves for self-support. And this work seems attended with no peculiar difficulty. The colored man is not a savage, to whom toil is torture, who has centered every idea of happiness and dignity in a wild freedom, who must exchange the boundless forest for a narrow plantation, and bend his proud neck to an unknown yoke. Labor was his first lesson, and he has been repeating it all his life. Can it be a hard task to teach him to labor for himself, to work from impulses in his own breast?

Much may be done at once to throw the slave on himself, to accustom him to work for his own and his family's support, to awaken forethought, and strengthen the habit of providing for the future. On every plantation there are slaves, who would do more for wages than from fear of punishment. There are those, who, if entrusted with a piece of ground, would support themselves and pay a rent in kind. There are those, who, if moderate task-work were given them, would gain their whole subsistence in their own time. Now every such man ought to be committed very much to himself. It is a crime to subject to the whip a man who can be made to toil from rational and honorable motives. This partial introduction of freedom would form a superior class among the slaves, whose example would have immense moral power on those who needed compulsion. The industrious and thriving would give an impulse to the whole race. It is important that the property, thus earned by the slave, should be made as sacred as that of any other member of the community, and for this end he should be enabled to obtain redress of wrongs. In case of being injured by his master in this or in any respect, he should either be set free, or, if unprepared for liberty, should be transferred to another guardian.

As another means of raising the slave and fitting him to act from higher motives than compulsion, a system of bounties and rewards should be introduced. New privileges, increased indulgences, honorable distinctions, expressions of respect, should be awarded to the honest and industrious. No people are more alive to commendation and honorable distinction than the colored race. Prizes for good conduct, adapted to their tastes and character, might in a good degree supersede the lash. Their love of ornament might be turned to a good account. The object is to bring the slave to labor from other motives than brutal compulsion. Such motives may easily be found, if the end be conscientiously proposed.

One of the great means of elevating the slave, and calling forth his energies, is to place his domestic relations on new ground. This is essential. We wish him to labor for his family. Then he must have a family to labor for. Then his wife and children must be truly his own. Then his home must be inviolate. Then the responsibilities of a husband and father must be laid on him. It is agreed he will be fit for freedom, as soon as the support of his family shall become his habit and his happiness; and how can he be brought to this condition, as long as he shall see no sanctity in the marriage-bond, as long as he shall see his wife and his children exposed to indignity and to sale, as long as their support shall not be entrusted to his care? No measure for preparing the slave for liberty can be so effectual as the improvement of his domestic lot. The whole power of religion should be employed to impress him with the sacredness and duties of marriage. The chaste and the faithful in this connexion should receive open and strong marks of respect. They should be treated as at the head of their race. The husband and wife, who prove false to each other, and who will not labor for their children, should be visited with the severest rebuke. To create a sense of domestic obligation, to awaken domestic affections, to give the means of domestic happiness, to fix deeply a conviction of the indissolubleness of marriage, and of the solemnity of the parental relation, these are the essential means of raising the slave to a virtuous and happy freedom. All other men labor for their families; and so will the slave, if the sentiments of a man be cherished in his breast. We keep him in bondage, because, if free, he will leave his wife and children to want; and this bondage breaks down all the feelings and habits which would incite him to toil for their support. Not a step will be taken towards the preparation of the slave for voluntary labor, till his domestic rights be respected. The violation of these, cries to God, more than any other evil of his lot.

To carry this and all other means of improvement into effect, it is essential that the slave should no longer be bought and sold. As long as he is made an article of merchandise, he cannot be fitted for the offices of a man. He will have little motive to accumulate comforts and ornaments to his hut, if at any moment he may be torn from it. While treated as property, he will have little encouragement to accumulate property, for it cannot be secure. While his wife and children may be exposed at auction, and carried, he knows not where, can he be expected to feel and act as a husband and father? It is time, that this Christian and civilized country should no longer be dishonored by one of the worst usages of barbarism. Break up the slave-market, and one of the chief obstructions to emancipation will be removed.

Let me only add, that religious instruction should go hand in hand with all other means for preparing the slave for freedom. The colored race are said to be peculiarly susceptible of the religious sentiment. If this be addressed wisely and powerfully, if the slave be brought to feel his relation and accountableness to God, and to comprehend the spirit of Christianity, he is fit for freedom. To accomplish this work, perhaps preaching should not be the only or chief instrument. Were the whole colored population to be assembled into Sunday-schools, and were the whites to become their teachers, a new and interesting relation would be formed between the races, and an influence be exerted which would do much to insure safety to the gift of freedom.

In these marks I have not intended to say that emancipation is an easy work, the work of a day, a good to be accomplished without sacrifices and toil. The colored man is, indeed, singularly susceptible of improvement, in consequence of the strength of his propensities to imitation and sympathy. But all great changes in society have their difficulties and inconveniences, and demand patient labor. I ask for no precipitate measures, no violent changes. I ask only that the slaveholding States would resolve conscientiously and in good faith to remove this greatest of moral evils and wrongs, and would bring immediately to the work all their intelligence, virtue, and power. That its difficulties would yield before such energies, who can doubt? Our weakness for holy enterprises lies generally in our own reluctant wills. Breathe into men a fervent purpose, and you awaken powers before unknown. How soon would slavery disappear, were the obligation to remove it thoroughly understood and deeply felt! We are told that the slaveholding States have recently prospered beyond all precedent. This accession to their wealth should be consecrated to the work of liberating their fellow-creatures.

Not one indulgence should be added to their modes of life, until the cry of the oppressed has ceased from their fields, until the rights of every human being are restored. Government should devote itself to this as its great object. Legislatures should meet to free the slave. The church should rest not, day or night, till this stain be wiped away. Let the deliberation of the wise, the energies of the active, the wealth of the prosperous, the prayers and toils of the good, have Emancipation for their great end. Let this be discussed habitually in the family circle, in the conference of Christians, in the halls of legislation. Let it mingle with the first thoughts of the slaveholder in the morning and the last at night. Who can doubt that to such a spirit God would reveal the means of wise and powerful action? There is but one obstacle to emancipation, and that is, the want of that spirit in which Christians and freemen should resolve to exterminate slavery.

I have said nothing of colonization among the means of removing slavery, because I believe that to rely on it for this object would be equivalent to a resolution to perpetuate the evil without end. Whatever good it may do abroad, and I trust it will do much, it promises little at home. If the slaveholding States, however, should engage in colonization, with a firm faith in its practicableness, with an energy proportionate to its greatness, and with a sincere regard to the welfare of the colored race, I am confident it will not fail from want of sympathy and aid on the part of the other States. In truth, these States will not withhold their hearts or hands from any well considered plan for the removal of slavery.

I have said nothing of the inconveniences and sufferings, which, it is urged, will follow emancipation, be it ever so safe; for these, if real, weigh nothing against the claims of justice. The most common objection is, that a mixture of the two races will be the result. Can this objection be urged in good faith? Can this mixture go on faster or more criminally than at the present moment? Can the slaveholder use the word " amalgamation" without a blush? Nothing, nothing, can arrest this evil but the raising of the colored woman to a new sense of character, to a new self-respect; and this she cannot gain but by being made free. That emancipation will have its evils we know; for all great changes, however beneficial, in the social condition of a people, must interfere with some interests, must bring loss or hardship to one class or another; but the evils of slavery exceed beyond measure the greatest which can attend its removal. Let the slaveholder desire earnestly, and in the spirit of self-sacrifice, to restore freedom, to secure the rights and the happiness of the slave, and a new light will break upon his path. "Every mountain of difficulty will be brought low, and the rough places be made smooth;" the means of duty will be become clear. But without this spirit, no eloquence of man or angel can persuade the slaveholder of the safety of emancipation.

CHAPTER VII.

ABOLITIONISM.

The word ABOLITIONIST in its true meaning comprehends every man who feels himself bound to exert his influence for removing slavery. It is a name of honorable import, and was worn, not long ago, by such men as Franklin and Jay. Events, however, continually modify terms; and of late, the word ABOLITIONIST has been narrowed from its original import, and restricted to the members of associations formed among us to promote Immediate Emancipation. It is not without reluctance that 1 give up to a small body a name which every good man ought to bear. But to make myself intelligible and to avoid circumlocution, I shall use the word in what is now its common acceptation.

I approach this subject unwillingly, because it will be my duty to censure those whom at this moment I would on no account hold up to public displeasure. The persecutions, which the abolitionists have suffered and still suffer, awaken only my grief and indignation, and incline me to defend them to the full extent which truth and justice will admit. To the persecuted of whatever name my sympathies are pledged, and especially to those who are persecuted in a cause substantially good. I would not for worlds utter a word to justify the violence recently offered to a party, composed very much of men blameless in life, and holding the doctrine of nonresistance to injuries; and of women, exemplary in their various relations, and acting, however mistakingly, from benevolent and pious impulses.

Of the abolitionists I know very few; but I am bound to say of these, that I honor them for their strength of principle, their sympathy with their fellow-creatures, and their active goodness. As a party, they are singularly free from political and religious sectarianism, and have been distinguished by the absence of management, calculation and worldly wisdom. That they have ever proposed or desired insurrection or vio- lence among the slaves there is no reason to believe. All their principles repel the supposition. It is a remarkable fact, that, though the South and the North have been leagued to crush them, though they have been watched by a million of eyes, and though prejudice has been prepared to detect the slightest sign of corrupt communication with the slave, yet this crime has not been fastened on a single member of this body. A few individuals at the South have, indeed, been tortured or murdered by enraged multitudes, on the charge of stirring up revolt; but their guilt and their connexion with the aboliti- onists were not, and from the circumstances and the nature of the case could not be, established by those deliberate and regular modes of investigation, which are necessary to an impartial judgment. Crimes, detected and hastily punished by the multitude in a moment of feverish suspicion and wild alarm, are generally creatures of fear and passion. The act which caused the present explosion of popular feeling was the sending of pamphlets by the Abolitionists into the slavehold- ing States. In so doing, they acted weakly and without de- corum; but they must have been insane, had they intended to stir up a servile war; for the pamphlets were sent, not by stealth, but by the public mail; and not to the slaves, but to their masters; to men in public life, to men of the greatest influence and distinction. Strange incendiaries these! They flourished their fire-brands about at noon-day; and, still more, put them into the hands of the very men whom it is said they wished to destroy. They are accused, indeed, of having sent some of the pamphlets to the free colored people, and if so, they acted with great and culpable rashness. But the publicity of the whole transaction absolves them of corrupt design.

The charge of corrupt design, so vehemently brought against the abolitionists, is groundless. The charge of fanaticism I have no desire to repel. But in the present age it will not do to deal harshly with the characters of fanatics. They form the mass of the people. Religion and Politics, Philanthropy and Temperance, Nullification and Antimasonry, the Level- ling Spirit of the man of business, all run into fanaticism.

This is the type of all our epidemics. A sober man who can find? The abolitionists have but caught the fever of the day. That they should have escaped it would have been a moral miracle.—I offer these remarks simply from a sense of justice. Had not a persecution, without parallel in our country, broken forth against the society, I should not have spoken a word in their defence. But whilst I have power I owe it to the Persecuted. If they have laid themselves open to the laws, let them suffer. For all their errors and sins let the tribunal of public opinion inflict the full measure of rebuke which they deserve. I ask no favor for them. But they shall not be stripped of the rights of man, of rights guarantied by the laws and Constitutions, without one voice, at least, being raised in their defence.

The abolitionists have done wrong, I believe; nor is their wrong to be winked at, because done fanatically or with good intention; for how much mischief may be wrought with good design! They have fallen into the common error of enthusiasts, that of exaggerating their object, of feeling as if no evil existed but that which they opposed, and as if no guilt could be compared with that of countenancing or upholding it. The tone of their newspapers, as far as I have seen them, has often been fierce, bitter, and abusive. Their imaginations have fed on pictures of the cruelty to which the slave is exposed, till they have seemed to think that his abode was perpetually resounding with the lash, and ringing with shrieks of agony; and accordingly, the slaveholder has been held up to execration, as a monster of cruelty. I know that many of their publications have been calm, well considered, and abounding in strong reasoning. But those, which have been most widely scattered and are most adapted to act on the common mind, have had a tone unfriendly both to manners and to the spirit of our religion. I doubt not that the majority of the abolitionists condemn the coarseness and violence of which I complain. But in this, as in most associations, the many are represented and controlled by the few, and are made to sanction and become responsible for what they disapprove.

One of their errors has been the adoption of " Immediate Emancipation" as their motto. To this they owe not a little of their unpopularity. This phrase has contributed much to spread far and wide the belief, that they wished immediately

to free the slave from all his restraints. They made explanations; but thousands heard the motto who never saw the
explanation; and it is certainly unwise for a party to choose
a watchword, which can be rescued from misapprehension
only by labored explication. It may also be doubted, whether they ever removed the objection which their language so
universally raised, whether they have not always recommend-
ed a precipitate action, inconsistent with the well-being of
the slave, and the order of the state.

Another objection to their movements is, that they have
sought to accomplish their objects by a system of Agitation;
that is, by a system of affiliated societies, gathered, and held
together, and extended, by passionate eloquence. This, in
truth, is the common mode by which all projects are now accomplished. The age of individual action is gone. Truth
cannot be heard unless shouted by a crowd. The weightiest
argument for a doctrine is the number which adopts it. Accordingly, to gather and organize multitudes is the first care
of him who would remove an abuse or spread a reform. That
the expedient is in some cases useful is not denied. But generally it is a showy, noisy mode of action, appealing to the
passions, and driving men into exaggeration; and there are
special reasons why such a mode should not be employed in
regard to slavery; for slavery is so to be opposed as not to
exasperate the slave, or endanger the community in which he
lives. The abolitionists might have formed an association;
but it should have been an elective one. Men of strong principles, judiciousness, sobriety, should have been carefully
sought as members. Much good might have been accomplished by the cooperation of such philanthropists. Instead
of this, the abolitionists, sent forth their orators, some of
them transported with fiery zeal, to sound the alarm against
slavery through the land, to gather together young and old,
pupils from schools, females hardly arrived at years of discretion, the ignorant, the excitable, the impetuous, and to organize these into associations for the battle against oppression.
Very unhappily they preached their doctrine to the colored
people, and collected these into their societies. To this mixed
and excitable multitude, minute, heartrending descriptions of
slavery were given in the piercing tones of passion; and slave-

F

holders were held up as monsters of cruelty and crime. Now to this procedure I must object as unwise, as unfriendly to the spirit of Christianity, and as increasing, in a degree, the perils of the slaveholding States. Among the unenlightened, whom they so powerfully addressed, was there not reason to fear that some might feel themselves called to subvert this system of wrong, by whatever means? From the free colored people this danger was particularly to be apprehended. It is easy for us to place ourselves in their situation. Suppose that millions of white men were enslaved, robbed of all their rights, in a neighbouring country, and enslaved by a black race, who had torn their ancestors from the shores on which our fathers. had lived. How deeply should we feel their wrongs! And would it be wonderful, if, in a moment of passionate excitement, some enthusiast should think it his duty to use his communication with his injured brethren for stirring them up to revolt?

Such is the danger from abolitionism to the slaveholding States. I know no other. It is but justice to add, that the principle of nonresistance, which the abolitionists have connected with their passionate appeals, seems to have counteracted the peril. I know not a case in which a member of an anti-slavery society has been proved by legal investigation to have tampered with the slaves; and after the strongly pronounced and unanimous opinion of the free States on the subject, this danger may be considered as having passed away. Still a mode of action, requiring these checks, is open to strong objections, and ought to be abandoned. Happy will it be, if the disapprobation of friends, as well as of foes, should give to abolitionists a caution and moderation, which would secure the acquiescence of the judicious, and the sympathies of the friends of mankind! Let not a good cause find its chief obstruction in its defenders. Let the truth, and the whole truth be spoken without paltering or fear; but so spoken as to convince, not inflame, as to give no alarm to the wise, and no needless exasperation to the selfish and passionate.

I know it is said, that nothing can be done but by excitement and vehemence; that the zeal which dares every thing is the only power to oppose to long rooted abuses. But it is not true that God has committed the great work of reforming the world to passion. Love is a minister of good only when it gives energy to the intellect, and allies itself with wisdom. The abolitionists often speak of Luther's vehemence as a model to future reformers. But who, that has read history, does not know that Luther's reformation was accompanied by tremendous miseries and crimes, and that its progress was soon arrested? and is there not reason to fear, that the fierce, bitter, persecuting spirit, which he breathed into the work, not only tarnished its glory, but limited its power? One great principle, which we should lay down as immovably true, is, that if a good work cannot be carried on by the calm, self-controlled, benevolent spirit of Christianity, then the time for doing it has not come. God asks not the aid of our vices. He can overrule them for good, but they are not the chosen instruments of human happiness.

We, indeed, need zeal, fervent zeal, such as will fear no man's power, and shrink before no man's frown, such as will sacrifice life to truth and freedom. But this energy of will ought to be joined with deliberate wisdom and universal charity. It ought to regard the whole, in its strenuous efforts for a part. Above all, it ought to ask first, not what means are most effectual, but what means are sanctioned by the Moral Law and by Christian Love. We ought to think much more of walking in the right path than of reaching our end. We should desire virtue more than success. If by one wrong deed we could accomplish the liberation of millions, and in no other way, we ought to feel that this good, for which, perhaps, we had prayed with an agony of desire, was denied us by God, was reserved for other times and other hands. The first object of a true zeal is, not that we may prosper, but that we may do right, that we may keep ourselves unspotted from every evil thought, word, and deed. Under the inspiration of such a zeal, we shall not find in the greatness of an enterprise an apology for intrigue or for violence. We shall not need immediate success to spur us to exertion. We shall not distrust God, because he does not yield to the cry of human impatience. We shall not forsake a good work, because it does not advance with a rapid step. Faith in truth, virtue, and Almighty Goodness, will save us alike from rashness and despair.

In lamenting the adoption by the abolitionists of the system of agitation by extensive excitement, I do not mean to condemn this mode of action as only evil. There are cases to which it is adapted; and, in general, the impulse which it gives is better than the selfish, sluggish indifference to good objects, into which the multitude so generally fall. But it must not supersede or be compared with Individual action. The enthusiasm of the Individual in a good cause is a mighty power. The forced, artificially excited enthusiasm of a multitude, kept together by an organization which makes them the instruments of a few leading minds, works superficially, and often injuriously. I fear that the native, noble-minded enthusiast often loses that single-heartedness which is his greatest power, when once he strives to avail himself of the machinery of associations. The true power of a Reformer lies in speaking truth purely from his own soul, without changing one tone for the purpose of managing or enlarging a party. Truth, to be powerful, must speak in her own words, and in no other's, must come forth with the authority and spontaneous energy of inspiration from the depths of the soul. It is the voice of the Individual giving utterance to the irrepressible conviction of his own thoroughly moved spirit, and not the shout of a crowd, which carries truth far into other souls, and insures it a stable empire on earth. For want of this, most which is now done, is done superficially. The progress of society depends chiefly on the honest inquiry of the Individual into the particular work ordained him by God, and on his simplicity in following out his convictions. This moral independence is mightier, as well as holier, than the practice of getting warm in crowds, and of waiting for an impulse from multitudes. The moment a man parts with moral independence; the moment he judges of duty, not from the inward voice, but from the interests and will of a party; the moment he commits himself to a leader or a body, and winks at evil, because division would hurt the cause; the moment he shakes off his particular responsibility, because he is but one of a thousand or million by whom the evil is done; that moment he parts with his moral power. He is shorn of the energy of singlehearted faith in the Right and the True. He hopes from man's policy what nothing but loyalty to God can accomplish. He substitutes coarse weapons forged by man's wisdom for celestial power.

The adoption of the common system of agitation by the abolitionists has proved signally unsuccessful. From the beginning it created alarm in the considerate, and strengthened the sympathies of the free States with the slaveholder. It made converts of a few individuals, but alienated multitudes. Its influence at the South has been evil without mixture. It has stirred up bitter passions and a fierce fanaticism, which have shut every ear and every heart against its arguments and persuasions. These effects are the more to be deplored, because the hope of freedom to the slave lies chiefly in the dispositions of his master. The abolitionist proposed, indeed, to convert the slaveholders ; and for this end he approached them with vituperation, and exhausted on them the vocabulary of abuse ! And he has reaped as he sowed. His vehement pleadings for the slaves have been answered by wilder ones from the slaveholder ; and, what is worse, deliberate defences of slavery have been sent forth, in the spirit of the dark ages, and in defiance of the moral convictions and feelings of the Christian and civilized world. Thus, with good purposes, nothing seems to have been gained. Perhaps (though I am anxious to repel the thought) something has been lost to the cause of freedom and humanity.

I earnestly desire that abolitionism may lay aside the form of public agitation, and seek its end by wiser and milder means. I desire as earnestly, and more earnestly, that it may not be put down by lawless force. There is a worse evil than abolitionism, and that is the suppression of it by lawless force. No evil greater than this can exist in the State, and this is never needed. Be it granted, that it is the design, or direct, palpable, tendency of abolitionism, to stir up insurrection at the South, and that no existing laws can meet the exigency. It is the solemn duty of the Chief Magistrate of the State to assemble immediately the legislative bodies, and their duty immediately to apply the remedy of Law. Let every friend of freedom, let every good man lift up his voice against mobs. Through these lies our road to tyranny. It is these which have spread the opinion, so common at the South, that the free States cannot long sustain republican institutions. No man seems awake to their inconsistency with liberty. Our whole phraseology is in fault. Mobs call themselves, and are called, the People, when in truth they assail immediately the sovereignty of the People, involve the guilt of usurpation and rebellion against the People. It is the fundamental principle of our institutions, that the People is Sovereign. But by the People we mean not an individual here and there, not a knot of twenty or a hundred or a thousand individuals in this or that spot, but the community formed into a body politic, and expressing and executing its will through regularly appointed organs. There is but one expression of the will or Sovereignty of the People, and this is Law. Law is the voice, the living act of the People. It has no other. When an individual suspends the operation of Law, resists its established ministers, and forcibly substitutes for it his own will, he is a usurper and a rebel. The same guilt attaches to a combination of individuals. These whether many or few, in forcibly superseding public law and establishing their own, rise up against the People, as truly as a single usurper. The People should assert its insulted majesty, its menaced sovereignty, in one case as decidedly as in the other. The difference between the mob and the individual is, that the usurpation of the latter has a permanence not easily given to the tumultuory movements of the former. The distinction is a weighty one. Little importance is due to sudden bursts of the populace, because they so soon pass away. But when mobs are organized, as in the French Revolution, or when they are deliberately resolved on and systematically resorted to, as the means of putting down an odious party, they lose this apology. A conspiracy exists against the Sovereignty of the People, and ought to be suppressed, as among the chief evils of the state.

In this part of the country our abhorrence of mobs is lessened by the fact, that they were thought to do good service in the beginning of the Revolution. They probably were useful then; and why? The work of that day was Revolution. To subvert a government was the fearful task to which our fathers thought themselves summoned. Their duty they believed was Insurrection. In such a work mobs had their place. The government of the State was in the hands of its foes. The people could not use the regular organs of administration, for these were held and employed by the power which they wished to crush. Violent, irregular efforts belonged to that day of convulsion. To resist and subvert institutions is the very work of mobs; and when these institutions are popular, when their sole end is to express and execute the will of the People, then mobs are rebellion against the People, and as such should be understood and suppressed. A people is never more insulted than when a mob takes its name. Abolition must not be put down by lawless force. The attempt so to destroy it ought to fail. Such attempts place abolitionism on a new ground. They make it, not the cause of a few enthusiasts, but the cause of freedom. They identify it with all our rights and popular institutions. If the Constitution and the laws cannot put it down, it must stand; and he who attempts its overthrow by lawless force is a rebel and usurper. The Supremacy of Law and the Sovereignty of the People are one and indivisible. To touch the one is to violate the other. This should be laid down as a first principle, an axiom, a fundamental article of faith which it must be heresy to question. A newspaper, which openly or by inuendoes excites a mob, should be regarded as sounding the tocsin of insurrection. On this subject the public mind slumbers, and needs to be awakened, lest it sleep the sleep of death.

How obvious is it, that pretexts for mobs will never be wanting, if this disorganizing mode of redressing evils be in any case allowed! We all recollect, that when a recent attempt was made on the life of the President of the United States, the cry broke forth from his friends, "that the assassin was instigated by the continual abuse poured forth on this distinguished man, and especially by the violent speeches uttered daily in the Senate of the United States." Suppose, now, that his adherents, to save the Chief Magistrate from murder, and to guard his constitutional advisers, had formed themselves into mobs, to scatter the meetings of his opponents. And suppose that they had resolved to put to silence the legislators, who, it was said, had abused their freedom of speech to blacken the character and put in peril the life of the Chief Magistrate. Would they not have had a better pretext than mobs against abolition? Was not assassination attempted? Had not the President received letters threatening his life unless he would change his measures? Can a year or a month pass, which will not afford equally grave reasons for insurrections of the populace? A system of mobs and a free government cannot stand together. The men who incite the former, and especially those who organize them, are among the worst enemies of the state. Of their motives I do not speak. They may think themselves doing service to their country, for there is no limit to the delusions of the times. I speak only of the nature and tendency of their actions. They should be suppressed at once by law, and by the moral sentiment of an insulted people.

In addition to all other reasons, the honor of our nation, and the cause of free institutions should plead with us to de- fend the laws from insult, and social order from subversion. The moral influence and reputation of our country are fast declining abroad. A letter, recently received from one of the most distinguished men of the continent of Europe, expresses the universal feeling on the other side of the ocean. After speaking of the late encroachments on liberty in France, he says, "On your side of the Atlantic, you contribute, also, to put in peril the cause of liberty. We did take pleasure in thinking that there was at least in the New World a country, where liberty was well understood, where all rights were gua- ranteed, where the people was proving itself wise and virtuous. For some time past, the news we receive from America is dis- couraging. In all your large cities we see mobs after mobs, and all directed to an odious purpose. When we speak of liberty, its enemies reply to us by *pointing to America*." The perse- cuted abolitionists have the sympathies of the civilized world. The country which persecutes them is covering itself with disgrace, and filling the hearts of the friends of freedom with fear and gloom. Already despotism is beginning to rejoice in the fulfilment of its prophesies, in our prostrated laws and dying liberties. Liberty is, indeed, threatened with death in a country, where any class of men are stripped with impunity of their constitutional rights. All rights feel the blow. A community, giving up any of its citizens to oppression and violence, invites the chains which it suffers others to wear.

CHAPTER VIII.

A few words remain to be spoken in relation to the duties of the Free States. These need to feel the responsibilities and dangers of their present position. The country is approaching a crisis on the greatest question which can be proposed to it, a question not of profit or loss, of tariffs or banks, or any temporary interests, but a question involving the First Principles of freedom, morals, and religion. Yet who seems to be awake to the solemnity of the present moment? Who seems to be settling for himself the great fundamental truths, by which private efforts and public measures are to be determined?

The North has duties to perform towards the South and towards itself. Let it resolve to perform them faithfully, impartially; asking first for the Right, and putting entire confidence in Well-doing. The North is bound to suppress all attempts of its citizens, should such be threatened, to excite insurrection at the South, all attempts to tamper with and to dispose to violence the minds of the slaves. The severest laws which consist with civilization may justly be resorted to for this end, and they should be strictly enforced. I believe, indeed, that there is no special need for new legislation on the subject. I believe that there was never a moment, when the slaveholding States had so little to apprehend from the free, when the moral feeling of the community in regard to the crime of instigating revolt was so universal, thorough, and inflexible, as at the present moment. Still, if the South needs other demonstrations than it now has of the moral and friendly spirit which in this respect pervades the North, let them be given. Still more, it is the duty of the free States to act by opinion, where they cannot act by law, to discountenance a system of agitation, on the subject of slavery, to frown on passionate appeals

to the ignorant, and on indiscriminate and inflammatory vituperation of the slaveholder. This obligation, also, has been
and will be fulfilled. There was never a stronger feeling
of responsibility in this particular than at the present moment.

There are, however, other duties of the free States, to which
they *may* prove false, and which they are too willing to forget.
They are bound, not in their public, but individual capacities,
to use every virtuous influence for the abolition of slavery.
They are bound to encourage that manly, moral, religious
discussion of it, through which strength will be given to the
continually increasing opinion of the civilized and Christian
world in favor of personal freedom. They are bound to seek
and hold the truth in regard to human rights, to be faithful
to their principles in conversation and conduct, never, never
to surrender them to private interest, convenience, flattery,
or fear.

The duty of being true to our principles is not easily to be
performed. At this moment an immense pressure is driving
the North from its true ground. God save it from imbecility,
from treachery to freedom and virtue! I have certainly no
feelings but those of good-will towards the South; but I
speak the universal sentiment of this part of the country, when
I say, that the tone which the South has often assumed towards the North has been that of a superior, a tone unconsciously borrowed from the habit of command, to which it is
unhappily accustomed by the form of its society. I must add,
that this high bearing of the South has not always been met
by a just consciousness of equality, a just self respect at the
North. The causes I will not try to explain. The effect I
fear is not to be denied. It is said, that those, who have
represented the North in Congress, have not always represented its dignity, its honor; that they have not always stood
erect before the lofty bearing of the South. Here lies our
danger. The North will undoubtedly be just to the South.
It must also be just to itself. This is not the time for syco-
phancy, for servility, for compromise of principle, for forget-
fulness of our rights, It is the time to manifest the spirit of
Men, a spirit which prizes, more than life, the principles
of liberty, of justice, of humanity, of pure morals, of pure
religion.

Let it not be thought that I would recommend to the North, what in some parts of our country is called " Chivalry," a spirit of which the duelling pistol is the best emblem, and which settles controversies with blood. A Christian and civilized man cannot but be struck with the approach to barbarism, with the insensibility to true greatness, with the incapacity of comprehending the divine virtues of Jesus Christ, which mark what is called "chivalry." I ask not the man of the North to borrow it from any part of the country. But I do ask him to stand in the presence of this " chivalry" with the dignity of moral courage and moral independence. Let him, at the same moment, remember the courtesy and deference due to the differing opinions of others, and the sincerity and firmness due to his own. Let him understand the lofty position which he holds on the subject of slavery, and never descend from it for the purpose of soothing prejudice or disarming passion. Let him respect the safety of the South, and still manifest his inflexible adherence to the cause of human rights and personal freedom.

On this point I must insist, because I see the North giving way to the vehemence of the South. In some, perhaps many, of our recent "Resolutions," a spirit has been manifested, at which, if not we, our children will blush. Not long ago there were rumors, that some of our citizens wished to suppress by law all discussion, all expression of opinion on slavery, and to send to the South such members of our community as might be claimed as instigators of insurrection. Such encroachments on rights could not, of course, be endured. We are not yet so fallen. Some echoes of the old eloquence of liberty still come down to us from our fathers. Some inspirations of heroism and freedom still issue from the consecrated walls of Faneuil Hall. Were we to yield to such encroachments, would not the soil of new England, ·so long trodden by freemen, heave and quake under the steps of her degenerate sons ? We are not prepared for these. But a weak, yielding tone, for which we seem to be prepared, may be the beginning of concessions which we shall one day bitterly rue.

The means used at the South to bring the North to compliance seem to demand particular attention. I will not record the contemptuous language which has been thrown on the frugal and money-getting habits of New England, or the menaces which have been addressed to our cupidity, for the purpose of putting us to silence on the subject of slavery. Such language does in no degree move me. I only ask that we may give no ground for its application. We can easily bear it, if we do not deserve it. Our mother country has been called a nation of shopkeepers, and New England ought not to be provoked by the name. Only let us give no sanction to the opinion that our spirit is narrowed to our shops; that we place the art of bargaining above all arts, all sciences, accomplishments, and virtues; that rather than lose the fruits of the slave's labor we would rivet his chains; that sooner than lose a market we would make a shipwreck of honor; that sooner than sacrifice present gain we would break our faith to our fathers and our children, to our principles and our God. To resent or retaliate reproaches would be unwise and unchristian. The only revenge worthy of a good man is, to turn reproaches into admonitions against baseness, into incitements to a more generous virtue. New England has long suffered the imputation of a sordid, calculating spirit, of supreme devotion to gain. Let us show that we have principles, compared with which the wealth of the world is light as air. It is a common remark here, that there is not a community under heaven, through which there is so general a diffusion of intelligence and healthful moral sentiment as in New England. Let not the just influence of such a society be impaired by any act which would give to prejudice the aspect of truth.

The free States, it is to be feared, must pass through a struggle. May they sustain it as becomes their freedom! The present excitement at the South can hardly be expected to pass away, without attempts to wrest from them unworthy concessions. The tone in regard to slavery in that part of our country is changed. It is not only vehement, but more false than formerly. Once slavery was acknowledged as an evil. Now it is proclaimed to be a good. We have even been told, not by a handful of enthusiasts in private life, but by men in the highest station and of widest influence at the South, that slavery is the soil into which political freedom strikes its deepest roots, and that republican institutions are never so secure as when the laboring class is reduced to servitude.

Certainly, no assertion of the wildest abolitionist could give such a shock to the slaveholder, as this new doctrine is fitted to give to the people of the North. Liberty, with a slave for her pedestal, and with a chain in her hand, differs so entirely from that lovely vision, that benignant Divinity, to which we, like our fathers, have paid homage, that we cannot endure that both should be called by the same name. A doctrine, more wounding or insulting to the mechanics, farmers, laborers of the North than this strange heresy, cannot well be conceived. A doctrine more irreverent, more fatal to republican institutions, was never fabricated in the councils of despotism. It does not, however, provoke us. I recall it only to show the spirit in which slavery is upheld, and to remind the free States of the calm energy which they will need, to keep themselves true to their own principles of liberty.

There is a great dread in this part of the country, that the union of the States may be dissolved by the conflict about slavery. To avert this evil, every sacrifice should be made but that of honor, freedom, and principle. No one prizes the Union more than myself. Perhaps I may be allowed to say, that I am attached to it by no common love. Most men value the Union as a means; to me it is an end. Most would preserve it for the prosperity of which it is the instrument; I love and would preserve it for its own sake. Some value it as favoring public improvements, facilities of commercial exchange, &c.; I value these improvements and exchanges chiefly as favoring union. I ask of the General Government to unite us, to hold us together as brethren in peace; and I care little whether it does any thing else. So dear to me is union. It is our highest national interest. All the pecuniary sacrifices which it can possibly demand should be made for it. The politicians in some parts of our country, who are calculating its value, and are willing to surrender it, because they may grow richer by separation, seem to me bereft of reason. Still, if the union can be preserved only by the imposition of chains on speech and the press, by prohibition of discussion on a subject involving the most sacred rights and dearest interests of humanity, then union would be bought at too dear a rate; then it would be changed from a virtuous bond into a league of crime and shame. Language cannot easily do justice to our attachment to the Union. We will yield every thing to it but Truth, Honor, and Liberty. These we can never yield.

Let the free States be firm, but also patient, forbearing, and calm. From the slaveholder they cannot look for perfect self-control. From his position he would be more than man, were he to observe the bounds of moderation. The consciousness which tranquilizes the mind can hardly be his. On this subject he has always been sensitive to excess. Much exasperation is to be expected. Much should be borne. Every thing may be surrendered but our principles and our rights.

———

My work is done. I ask and hope for it the Divine blessing, as far as it expresses Truth, and breathes the spirit of Justice and Humanity. If I have written any thing under the influence of prejudice, passion, or unkindness to any human being, I ask forgiveness of God and man. I have spoken strongly, not to offend or give pain, but to produce in others deep convictions corresponding to my own. Nothing but a feeling, which I could not escape, of the need of such a work at this very moment has induced me to fix my thoughts on so painful a subject. The few last months have increased my solicitude for the country. Public sentiment has seemed to me to be losing its healthfulness and vigor. I have seen symptoms of the decline of the old spirit of liberty. Servile opinions have seemed to gain ground among us. The faith of our fathers in free institutions has waxen faint, and is giving place to despair of human improvements. I have perceived a disposition to deride abstract rights, to speak of freedom as a dream, and of republican governments as built on sand. I have perceived a faint-heartedness in the cause of human rights. The condemnation, which has been passed on abolitionists, has seemed to be settling into acquiescence in slavery. The sympathies of the community have been turned from the slave to the master. The impious doctrine, that human laws can repeal the Divine, can convert unjust and oppressive power into a moral right, has more and more tinctured the style of conversation and the press. With these sad and solemn views of society, I could not be silent; and I thank God, amidst the consciousness of great weakness and imperfection, that I have been able to offer this humble tribute, this sincere, though feeble, testimony, this expression of heartfelt allegiance, to the cause of Freedom, Justice, and Humanity.

Having stated the circumstances which have moved me to write, I ought to say, that they do not discourage me. Were darker omens to gather round us, I should not despair. With a faith like his, who came to prepare the way for the great Deliverer, I feel and can say, "The Kingdom of Heaven," the Reign of Justice and Disinterested Love, "is at hand, and All Flesh shall see the Salvation of God." I know, and rejoice to know, that a power, mightier than the prejudices and oppression of ages, is working on earth for the world's redemption, the power of Christian Truth and Goodness. It descended from heaven in the person of Christ. It was manifest in his life and death. From his cross it went forth conquering and to conquer. Its mission is "to preach deliverance to the captive, and to set at liberty them that are bound." It has opened many a prison-door. It is ordained to break every chain. I have faith in its triumphs. I do not, cannot despair.

NOTES.

NOTE I.

I WISH to add a few statements to show how little reliance can be placed on what seem to a superficial observer mitigations or advantages of slavery, and how much safer it is to argue from the experience of all times and from the principles of human nature, than from insulated facts.

I once passed a colored woman at work on a plantation, who was singing apparently with animation, and whose general manners would have led me to set her down as the happiest of the gang. I said to her, " Your work seems pleasant to you." She replied, " No, Massa." Supposing that she referred to something particularly disagreeable in her immediate occupation, I said to her, " Tell me, then, what part of your work is most pleasant." She answered, with much emphasis, " *No part* pleasant. We *forced* to do it." These few words let me into the heart of the slave. I saw under its apparent lightness a human heart.

On this plantation, the most favored woman, whose life was the easiest, earnestly besought a friend of mine to buy her and put her in the way to earn her freedom. A daughter of this woman, very young, had fallen a victim to the manager of the estate. How far this cause influenced the exasperated mother I did not learn.

I heard of an estate managed by an individual who was considered as singularly successful, and who was able to govern the slaves without the use of the whip. I was anxious to see him, and trusted that some discovery had been made favorable to humanity. I asked him how he was able to dispense with corporal punishment. He replied to me, with a very determined look, " The slaves know that the work *must* be done, and that it is better to do it without punishment than with it." In other words, the certainty and dread of chastisement were so impressed on them that they never incurred it.

I then found that the slaves on this well managed estate decreased in number. I asked the cause. He replied, with perfect frankness and ease, " The gang is not large enough for the estate." In other words, they were not equal to the work of the plantation and yet were made to do it, though with the certainty of abridging life.

On this plantation the huts were uncommonly convenient. There was an unusual air of neatness. A superficial observer would have called the slaves happy. Yet they were living under a severe, subduing discipline, and were overworked to a degree that shortened life.

I cannot forget my feelings on visiting a hospital belonging to the plantation of a gentleman highly esteemed for his virtues, and whose manners and conversation expressed much benevolence and conscientiousness. When I entered with him the hospital, the first object on which my eye fell was a young woman, very ill, probably approaching death. She was stretched on the floor. Her head rested on something like a pillow but her body and limbs were extended on the hard boards. The owner, I doubt not, had at least as much kindness as myself; but he was so used to see the slaves living without common comforts, that the idea of unkindness in the present instance did not enter his mind.

The severest blow I ever saw given to a slave was inflicted by a colored driver on a young girl, who, on removing a load of wood from a horse, had let a stick fall against the animal's leg. I remonstrated with the man, as soon as an opportunity offered, against his inhumanity. He said, " Massa, I have the care of the horse, and the manager *lick me* if he get hurt." This answer explained to me the common remark, that the black drivers are more cruel than the whites. I saw where the cruelty *began*.

I once heard some slaves, who had been taken by law from their master, singing a song of their own composition, and at the end of every stanza they joined with a complaining tone in a chorus, of which the burden was, "We got no Massa." Here seemed a striking proof of attachment to the master; but on inquiry into the rest of the song, I found it was an angry repetition of the severities which they were suffering from the new superintendant. They wanted their master as an escape from cruelty.

Facts of this kind, which make no noise, which escape or mislead a casual observer, help to show the character of slavery more than occasional excesses of cruelty though these must be frequent. They show how deceptive are the appearances of good connected with it; and how much may be suffered under the manifestation of of much kindness. It is, in fact, next to impossible to estimate precisely the evils of slavery. The slave writes no books, and the slaveholder is too inured to the system, and too much interested in it to be able to comprehend it. Perhaps tho laws of the slave states are the most unexceptionable witnesses which we can obtain from that quarter; and the barbarity of these is decisive testimony against an institution which requires such means for its support.

NOTE II.

I think it right to state, that my views of abolitionism have been founded in part, perhaps chiefly, on the testimony of others. I have attended no abolition-meetings, and never heard an abolition-address. But the strong, and next to universal impression, in regard to the tendency of the operations of this party to inflame common minds, confirmed, as it is, by what I have seen of their newspapers, must be essentially true. The orator, who was chiefly employed in addressing their meetings and forming societies, was distinguished by his vehemence and passionate invectives. On one occasion, there is strong proof of his having given an opinion in favor of cruel vengeance on the part of the slaves. This seems to contradict what I have said of the steady inculcation of forbearance and non- resistance by the abolitionists. But this case if correctly reported, was an exception, an ebullition of uncontrollable passion in an individual, for which the rest were not responsible. I have thought it my duty to state the kind of evidence on which my views of abolitionism are founded, that others may better judge what confidence is due to them. In times of great excitement, it is not easy to arrive at the precise truth.

NOTE III.

It was my purpose to address a Chapter to the South, but the failure of strength compelled me to pause; and when I considered, that the circulation of my book in that part of the country might be a crime, I had no encouragement to proceed.

I beg, however, to say that nothing which I have written can have proceeded from unkind feeling toward the South; for in no other part of the country have my writings found a more gratifying reception; from no other part have I received stronger expressions of sympathy. To these I am certainly not insensible. My own feelings, had I consulted them, would have led me to stifle every expression, which could give pain to those from whom I have received nothing but good will.

I wished to suggest to the slaveholders, that the excitement now prevalent among themselves, was incomparably more perilous, more fitted to stir up insurrection, than all the efforts of abolitionists, allowing these to be ever so corrupt. I also wished to remind the men of principle and influence in that part of the country, of the necessity of laying a check on lawless procedures, in regard to the citizens of the North. We have heard of large subscriptions at the South for the apprehension of some of the abolitionists in the free States, and for the transportation of them to parts of the country where they would meet the fate, which, it is said, they deserve. Undoubtedly the respectable portion of the slaveholding communities are not answerable for these measures. But does not policy, as well as principle, require such men steadily to discountenance them? At present, the free States have stronger sympathies with the South than ever before. But can it be supposed that they will suffer their citizens to be stolen, exposed to violence, and murdered, by other States? Would not such an outrage rouse them to feel and act as one man? Would it not indentify the abolitionists with our most sacred rights? One kidnapped, murdered abolitionist would do more for the violent destruction of slavery than a thousand societies. His name would be sainted. The day of his death would be set apart for solemn heart-stirring commemoration. His blood would cry through the land with a thrilling voice, would pierce every dwelling, and find a response in every heart. Do men under the light of the present day, need to be told, that enthusiasm is not a flame to be quenched with blood? On this point, good and wise men, and the friends of the country at the North and South, can hold but one opinion; and if the press, which, I grieve to say, has kept an ominous silence amidst the violations of law and rights, would but speak plainly and strongly, the danger would be past.

Since writing the preceding chapters, I have seen in a newspaper some notice of a meeting of ministers in one of the Southern States, in which slavery was spoken of as sinful. If the account was correct, the liberty of speech is not every where denied to the degree to which I had supposed.

I have only to add, that I alone am responsible for what I have now written. I represent no society, no body of men, no part of the country. I have written by no one's instigation and with no one's encouragement, but solely from my own convictions. If offence is given I alone ought to bear it.

PRINTED BY E. C. OSBORNE, TEMPLE ROW, BIRMINGHAM.

For EU product safety concerns, contact us at Calle de José Abascal, 56–1°, 28003 Madrid, Spain or eugpsr@cambridge.org.

www.ingramcontent.com/pod-product-compliance
Ingram Content Group UK Ltd.
Pitfield, Milton Keynes, MK11 3LW, UK
UKHW012337130625
459647UK00009B/337